The Complete
Vegetarian Pasta
Cookbook

The Complete Vegetarian Pasta Cookbook

Over 150 Delicious and Nutritious Recipes
for the Discerning Vegetarian Cook

EDITED BY EMMA CALLERY

CHARTWELL
BOOKS, INC.

A QUINTET BOOK

Published by Chartwell Books A Division of
Book Sales, Inc.
114 Northfield Avenue
Edison, New Jersey 08837

This edition produced for sale in the U.S.A., its
territories and dependencies only.

Reprinted 1996 , 2004

ISBN 0–7858–0356–4

This book was designed and produced by
Quintet Publishing Limited
6 Blundell Street
London N7 9BH

Creative Director: Richard Dewing
Designer: Ian Hunt
Editor: Emma Callery
Editorial Assistant: Clare Hubbard

Typeset in Great Britain by
Central Southern Typesetters, Eastbourne
Manufactured by Eray Scan Pte Ltd, Singapore
Printed by Star Standard Industries (Pte) Ltd,
Singapore

Material in this book previously appeared in *The
Encyclopedia of Pasta* by Bridget Jones, *The Fresh
Pasta Cookbook* by Bridget Jones and the
Vegetarian Pasta Cookbook by Sarah Maxwell

Contents

Introduction

Pasta is a useful food to include in a well-balanced diet. In itself, it does not have a high fat content, it provides starch for energy, and it may include a small, but useful, source of protein. Egg pasta can make a valuable contribution of protein to a vegetarian diet where many different sources make up the total intake, unlike a diet based on fish, poultry, or meat where concentrated sources of animal protein are eaten regularly.

As pasta is often eaten with substantial salads, it can be a useful food for promoting healthy eating.

There are many excellent sauces and accompaniments that substantiate the image of pasta as a well-balanced, healthy food. However, there is also a distinct tendency to smother pasta with olive oil, butter, cream, and cheese, so it is up to us whether we eat it in a healthy or less healthy way.

PASTA FOR ENERGY: A CARBOHYDRATE FOOD

Primarily, pasta is a carbohydrate food, usually based on wheat. Its main contribution to diet is starch. Depending on the type, as we have seen, the pasta may also make a contribution of protein (not that protein is a nutrient lacking in the Western diet). It also provides some minerals and contributes a small amount of certain vitamins.

To put this into context, pasta is similar to potatoes or rice in its role in our diet. Starches should be the main source of energy in the diet (as opposed to sugars and fats). The body breaks down food to obtain energy. Simple sugars are most easily broken down, and starch, which does not have a high fiber content, is digested more quickly than foods that contain a significant amount of fiber.

ALL-IMPORTANT FIBER

Fiber is essential in the diet. White pasta is *not* a valuable source of fiber, but wholewheat pasta does provide a useful supply of dietary fiber, or non-starch polysaccharides, as the experts would like it termed.

PASTA AND FAT: COMPARISONS WITH ALTERNATIVES

Pasta is often promoted as a low-fat food. It does have a low-fat content in itself and, when olive oil is used in its manufacture, the greater percentage of the fat it does have, may be monounsaturated. Potatoes, rice, couscous, and wheat are also low-fat foods, and they may contain less fat than pasta.

For example, 4oz raw macaroni contains about 1.8g fat; a similar weight of raw potato contains 0.2g fat. As 4oz raw potato is hardly a representative portion, and 4oz macaroni is a generous portion, a better comparison is between 4oz raw macaroni with 1.8g fat and 12oz raw potato with 0.7g fat: the macaroni has more than double the quantity of fat than the potato.

This comparison can be made between egg noodles and various other types of pasta with similar indications. It is also interesting to compare pasta with rice. Rice has a higher fat content than potatoes, but it is lower than pasta.

PASTA AND CALORIE-CONTROLLED DIETS

Pasta is a useful food to eat when following a reduced-calorie or calorie-controlled diet because it provides reasonable bulk for its calorie content. The same is true of any food that has a high starch and low fat content, such as potatoes and rice.

One of the difficulties of promoting pasta as useful in low-calorie diets and when slimming is in distinguishing the low-calorie dishes with pasta from the others, which are calorific. For example, a hearty bowl of boiled pasta with steamed zucchini, tossed with fresh basil, and topped with 2 tbsp of grated Parmesan cheese, plenty of black pepper, and 1 tbsp of fromage frais is every slimmer's dream meal. However, the simpler alternative of pasta tossed with olive oil and garlic, and served with a bowl of Parmesan or pecorino to taste will provide a far higher calorie intake, quite out of the realms of the target for a low-calorie meal. So, it is all down to what you serve it with.

ABOVE *Tagliatelle with Grated Carrot and Green Onion*

CHAPTER ONE

MAKING PASTA

There is no great mystery involved in making simple, Italian-style pasta dough. All it takes is a touch of muscle power for the kneading and rolling — unless, of course, you have a pasta machine which will make light work of pounding the ingredients to a smooth, pliable dough. It really is worth making your own dough, if only for filled pasta such as tortellini and ravioli; apart from the variety of fillings which you can introduce, home-made filled pasta is infinitely superior to the average (or even slightly better) bought alternatives. Remember that you can make a large batch of shapes, fill them, and freeze them for future use.

The majority of the recipes in the chapters which follow do not necessarily need home-made pasta. Most large supermarkets offer a range of fresh pasta shapes which usually includes spirals or twists that you cannot make at home, egg noodles, spaghetti, lasagna, paglia e fieno, and fettucine. Flavored pasta doughs vary in quality — spinach dough (verdi) is popular and tastes good but some of the herb-flavored doughs taste inferior and, frankly, may ruin a good home-made sauce!

Equipment for Making Pasta

You do not need any special equipment for making pasta. A large area of work surface helps, but it is not essential as you can always roll the dough in two or more batches. A mixing bowl, spoon, and rolling pin are the basics, and an extra-long rolling pin is useful (make sure an ordinary one does not have knobs at the ends as they indent the dough and make rolling out difficult). You may also wish to invest in some of the following:

PASTRY WHEEL A fluted pastry wheel for cutting out ravioli.

RAVIOLI PAN A small metal pan with round or square hollows. Lay a sheet of pasta over the pan, press it in neatly and spoon mixture into the hollows. Brush with egg, cover with a second sheet of dough and roll the top to seal before cutting out the ravioli.

PASTA MACHINE A small but heavy metal machine for rolling pasta. Fitted with plain rollers which can be set at different distances apart,

this basic, inexpensive machine is terrific. Once the dough is briefly kneaded, rolling it through the machine several times on the widest setting will complete the kneading.

Set the rollers at the narrow width for rolling out sheets of dough or substitute cutting rollers to make noodles or spaghetti. A ravioli filler attachment makes very small, neat ravioli by feeding the pasta and filling through a hopper-like attachment.

ELECTRIC PASTA MACHINES Large, expensive machines are available for mixing, kneading, rolling, and extruding pasta. Unless you are an avid pasta eater, such a machine is an unlikely piece of equipment for the average domestic kitchen.

PASTA DRYER A small wooden rack on which to hang cut noodles or sheets of pasta as they are rolled out.

BELOW *Hand-turned pasta machine with attachments for filled pasta*

Pasta-Making Techniques

MIXING AND KNEADING

Unlike pastry, pasta dough needs a firm hand and a positive approach to mixing and kneading. The dough will seem very dry and prone to crumbling at first, but as you knead it the oil and egg combine fully with the flour, and the ingredients bind together.

1 Mix the ingredients in the bowl, using a spoon at first, then your hand.

2 Begin the kneading process in the bowl, bringing any dough together and "wiping" the bowl clean of any crumbs.

3 Place the dough on a lightly floured, clean surface and knead it into a ball. Add a little flour to the work surface to prevent the dough sticking, but try to keep this to a minimum during kneading.

4 Once the dough has come together, knead it firmly and rhythmically, pressing it down and out in one movement, then pulling the edge of the dough back in toward the middle in the next movement. Keep turning the dough as you knead it, so that you work it around in a circle rather than constantly pressing and pulling one side. Keep the dough moving and it will not stick to the surface.

5 The dough is ready when it is smooth and warm. Wrap it in a plastic bag or plastic wrap and set it aside for 15–30 minutes if possible before rolling it out.

ABOVE *Kneading pasta dough.*

ROLLING OUT

When rolling the dough, try to keep it in the shape you want to end up with. Press the dough flat, forming it into an oblong or square, then roll it out firmly. Lift and "shake out" the dough a few times initially to insure it does not stick to the surface. As the dough becomes thinner, you have to handle it more carefully to avoid splitting it. However, pasta dough is far more durable than pastry and the smoother it becomes as it is rolled, the tougher it is. It can be rolled out very thinly – until you can almost see through it – without breaking, but this is not essential for the majority of pasta dishes. Dust the surface under the dough with a little flour occasionally, as necessary, and dust the top, rubbing the flour over the dough with one hand. Continue rolling until the dough is thin and even – a common mistake is to leave the dough too thick, so that it becomes unpleasantly solid when cooked. For noodles, or pasta which is to be eaten plain or topped with sauce, try to roll out to the thickness of a piece of brown wrapping paper: this makes excellent noodles.

Make sure the surface under the dough is sifted with flour, then cover the dough completely with plastic wrap and leave for 10 minutes. This relaxes the dough before cutting – it is not essential but does prevent the dough from shrinking as it is cut.

ABOVE *Rolling out pasta dough.*

MAKING PASTA

CUTTING PASTA

You need a large, sharp knife and a large floured platter or tray on which to place the pasta (a clean roasting pan will do). Flour the dough lightly before cutting. Once cut, keep the pasta dusted with flour to prevent it sticking together. Pasta may be dried before cooking by hanging it on a rack or spreading it out. I have, before now, draped pasta between two chair backs (covering them with paper towels first). To be honest, I have not found any great advantage to drying the pasta and have always felt that it is thoroughly inconvenient and unhygienic. It seems to cook well if it is added to boiling water straight after rolling.

SHEETS Trim the dough edges so that they are straight, then cut the pasta into squares or oblongs. This is basic lasagna, so cut the dough to suit the size of dish.

NOODLES Dust the dough well with flour, then roll it up. Use a sharp knife to cut the roll into ¼in wide slices. Shake out the slices as they are cut and they fall into long noodles. Keep the noodles floured and loosely piled on the tray to prevent them from sticking together. Cover loosely with plastic wrap.

CIRCLES OR SHAPES Use cookie cutters and chocolate cutters to stamp out circles and shapes.

SQUARES Trim the dough edges, then use a clean, long ruler to cut the dough into wide strips. Cut these across into squares.

SMALL SQUARES Use a ruler to cut the dough into 1in wide strips, then cut these across into squares. The small squares may be cooked and treated as bought pasta shapes.

OTHER SHAPES If you have the time, you can make other shapes by hand. Cut the dough into strips, then into small oblongs or squares. By twisting, pleating, or pinching you can make bows and funny little twists and, I am sure, lots of clever alternatives. Frankly, I feel inclined to leave this to the manufacturers as it is very time-consuming.

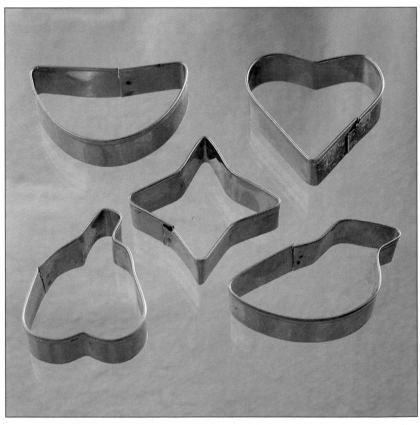

ABOVE *Cookie and chocolate cutters.*

ABOVE *Pasta shapes made with cookie cutters.*

RIGHT *Home-made fresh pasta squares*

COOKING FRESH PASTA

Pasta should be cooked in enormous quantities of boiling water. Although you can get away with less water than the volume which is always suggested for authentic recipes (which means using a stock pot or catering-size kettle when cooking enough for four people), you need a large saucepan which holds 5–6 quarts to cook ¾–1lb of pasta. If you have a stock pot or very large pressure cooker which you can use without the lid on, so much the better.

Pour water into the pan to three-quarters of its capacity. Add salt and bring the water to a boil. Adding a little oil to the water helps to prevent it from frothing on the surface and boiling over rapidly – the pasta will not stick together if you have a pan that is large enough, and adding oil does little to prevent the pasta sticking in a pan that is too small! Add the pasta when the water is fully boiling, stir it, and bring the water back to a boil rapidly. Be ready to turn down the heat, otherwise the water will froth over. Cook for about 3 minutes for noodles and other types of unfilled pasta. Filled pasta requires longer to allow the filling to cook through.

When cooked, the pasta should be "al dente" (with bite). It should be firm yet tender, not soft or sticky. Drain the cooked pasta at once, pouring it into a large colander. Shake the colander over the sink, then tip the pasta into a hot bowl and add the dressing or sauce. Serve at once. Chill leftover pasta in a covered container. Reheat in the microwave or in a sauce on the stove or in the oven.

CHILLING PREPARED PASTA

Dust the pasta with plenty of flour and place it in a large airtight container in the refrigerator. Cook within 2 days of making or freeze promptly. The unrolled dough may be wrapped and chilled for 1–2 days.

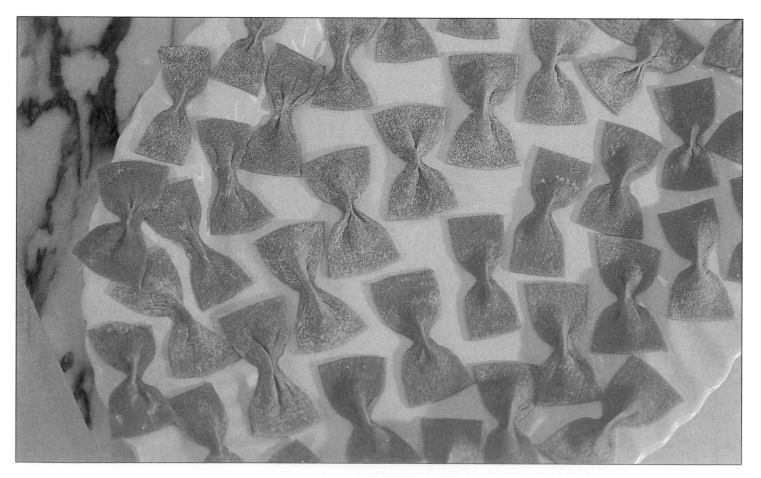

ABOVE *Homemade fresh pasta bows*

FREEZING PASTA

Uncooked fresh pasta freezes very well but it is best to roll and cut the dough first. Separate sheets of pasta by interleaving waxed paper between them. Flour noodles and pack them loosely in plastic bags, then spread them out fairly flat for freezing, so they do not form a lump. Bought fresh pasta is an excellent freezer candidate that is ideal for impromptu meals.

Do not thaw frozen pasta before cooking, simply add it to boiling water and cook as for fresh pasta. Noodles and most other shapes take about the same time to cook as unfrozen pasta, once the water has come to the boil again. Frozen filled pasta requires extra cooking time to allow the filling to thaw and cook properly.

Cooked lasagna and cannelloni or similar layered pasta dishes freeze well but cooked shapes and noodles tend to have an inferior texture if frozen after cooking.

USING THE RECIPES
★ Oven temperatures refer to conventional ovens; if you have a forced convection oven, please refer to the manufacturer's instructions for adapting cooking times or temperatures.

★ Unless otherwise stated, herbs are fresh, not dried.

★ Eggs are medium-size unless otherwise stated.

ABOVE *Fresh pasta noodles ready for freezing*

ABOVE *Commercial pasta production, Italian style*

Pasta Dough

MAKES ABOUT 1¼lb PASTA

3 cups all-purpose flour
1 tsp salt
3 eggs
¼ cup olive oil
1 tbsp water

1 Mix the flour and salt together in a large bowl. Make a well in the middle, then add the eggs, olive oil, and water. Use a spoon to mix the eggs, oil, and water, gradually working in the flour. When the mixture begins to bind into clumps, scrape the spoon clean and knead the dough together with your hands.

2 Press the dough into a ball and roll it around the bowl to leave the bowl completely clean of the mixture. Then place the dough on a lightly floured, clean surface and knead it thoroughly until it is smooth. Follow the notes on kneading (see page 11), keeping the dough moving and adding the minimum extra flour required to prevent it sticking as you work.

3 Wrap the dough in a plastic bag and leave it to rest for 15–30 minutes before rolling it out. Do not chill the dough as this will make it difficult to handle.

ABOVE *Mixing the dough*

ABOVE *Kneading the dough*

FLAVORED PASTA

The following may be used with the above recipe.

BEET Puree 2oz cooked and peeled beet with 2 eggs in a food processor or blender, or press it through a strainer (this eliminates dark speckles). Add the beet puree with the remaining egg. Omit the oil and water. Do not use beet that has been preserved in acetic acid or vinegar: it must be freshly boiled or the untreated vacuum-packed type.

CARROT Omit half the oil and water but add 2 tbsp carrot juice with the eggs. Pure carrot juice is available from natural food stores and delicatessens.

HERB Add ¼ cup chopped mixed fresh herbs to the flour and salt. Suitable herbs include parsley, thyme, sage, tarragon, chives, chervil, marjoram, and fennel. Rosemary may be used but only in very small quantities as it is a strongly flavored herb. Balance the delicate herbs against the stronger ones by using less of the latter. Use two, three, or more herbs but remember that a delicate herb like dill will be totally lost if combined with many other herbs. Dill is best mixed with chives and a little parsley.

OLIVE Finely chop 1 cup black olives and add them to the flour.

SPINACH Wash and trim ½lb fresh spinach. Place the damp leaves in a saucepan. Cover tightly and cook over high heat for 5 minutes, shaking the pan often. Place the spinach in a strainer placed over a bowl. Press and squeeze all the juice from the spinach, leaving the leaves as dry as possible. Add ⅓ cup spinach juice to the pasta and omit the oil and water.

TOMATO Add 1 tbsp concentrated tomato paste, beating it into the eggs.

TURMERIC Add 1 tbsp ground turmeric to the flour. For a pleasing, unusual, lightly spiced pasta, add 1 tbsp white cumin seeds to the flour with the turmeric.

WALNUT Use walnut oil instead of olive oil.

ABOVE *Fresh flavored noodles*

ABOVE *Dried flavored shapes*

Cheese Sauce

This sauce will keep in the refrigerator for up to a week. Use for lasagnas, bakes, toppings, and fillings.

MAKES ABOUT 2½ CUPS

2 tbsp butter or margarine
¼ cup all-purpose flour
2½ cups warm milk
1 tsp Dijon mustard
1 cup grated, mature Cheddar cheese
salt and freshly ground black pepper

1 Melt the butter or margarine in a medium-sized saucepan, and stir in the flour. Cook for 30 seconds, then remove from the heat.

2 Stir in the milk, a little at a time, blending well after each addition to prevent any lumps. Return the sauce to a medium heat, and stir constantly until the sauce thickens and boils.

3 Add the mustard and cheese, and season to taste with salt and freshly ground black pepper. Continue to cook, stirring constantly, until the cheese has melted.

VARIATIONS

MUSHROOM SAUCE Omit the mustard and cheese, and stir in ⅓lb chopped button mushrooms that have been sauteed in a little olive oil with a clove of crushed garlic and a pinch of dried thyme.

TOMATO SAUCE Omit the mustard and cheese and stir in 3 tbsp tomato paste.

White Sauce

Well-cooked, good-quality pasta makes a delicious meal with the minimum of additions: in the Italian kitchen that means olive oil and garlic or butter with parmesan or a creamy milk-based sauce. White sauce is a basic milk sauce which is lightly flavored with bay and mace.

MAKES ABOUT 2½ CUPS

1 thick onion slice
1 bay leaf
1 mace blade
2 parsley sprigs
2½ cups milk
3 tbsp butter
⅓ cup all-purpose flour
salt and freshly ground black pepper

1 Place the onion, bay leaf, mace, and parsley in a saucepan. Add the milk and heat slowly until just boiling. Remove from the heat, cover, and leave for 45 minutes.

2 Strain the milk into a measuring cup. Wash the saucepan, then melt the butter and stir in the flour. Slowly pour in the milk, stirring all the time. Continue stirring until the sauce boils, then reduce the heat, if necessary, so that it just simmers. Cook for 3 minutes, stirring occasionally. Add seasoning to taste.

3 If the sauce is not used straight away, lay a piece of dampened waxed paper directly on its surface to prevent a skin forming.

Tomato Sauce

Good fresh pasta and a rich tomato sauce, topped with some freshly grated Parmesan cheese, is a simple yet splendid meal, particularly if there is a really fresh, crisp green salad as an accompaniment. This sauce also has many uses in baked dishes or with stuffed pasta.

SERVES 4–6

2 tbsp olive oil
1 large onion, chopped
1 carrot, chopped
1 celery stalk, chopped
1 garlic clove, crushed
1 bay leaf
2 thyme sprigs
4 parsley sprigs
1 tbsp all-purpose flour
2 tbsp tomato paste
2lb ripe tomatoes, roughly chopped
1 tbsp sugar
½ cup red wine
salt and freshly ground black pepper
freshly grated Parmesan cheese, to serve

1 Heat the oil in a large, heavy-based saucepan. Add the onion, carrot, celery, garlic, bay leaf, thyme, and parsley. Cook, stirring, for 10 minutes, until the onion is softened slightly but not browned.

2 Stir in the flour and tomato paste. Then add the tomatoes and sugar and stir in the wine. Add some seasoning, bring to a boil, and stir thoroughly. Reduce the heat, cover the pan, and leave to simmer for 1 hour.

3 Remove the bay leaf and herb sprigs, then puree the sauce in a blender and press it through a strainer to remove the seeds. Reheat and taste for seasoning before serving. Ladle the sauce over pasta and top with Parmesan cheese to taste.

Pesto Sauce

This traditional Italian sauce should be used in moderation as it has a very strong flavor. The texture of the pesto can be left relatively coarse or pureed until smooth.

SERVES 4–6

2 cloves of garlic, crushed
½ cup chopped, fresh basil
2 tbsp chopped, fresh parsley
½ cup pine nuts
1 cup freshly grated Parmesan cheese
½ cup extra virgin olive oil
salt and freshly ground black pepper

1 Place all the ingredients in a food processor or blender, and blend until the pesto reaches the desired texture.

2 Stir Pesto Sauce into freshly cooked pasta tossed in butter and freshly ground black pepper. Serve immediately with extra freshly grated Parmesan cheese.

> ### TIP
> For a more traditional method of preparation, place all the ingredients in a mortar and use the pestle to grind and pound until the pesto reaches the desired texture.

CHAPTER TWO

SOUPS

 This chapter aims to broaden the view that soup and pasta together spell just one thing — minestrone. All large supermarkets offer at least one or two types of soup pasta and you will find some clever miniature shapes in better Italian delicatessens. So, adding pasta to your favorite soup is a good way to make it even better.

Apart from the Italian soups, light Oriental soups also use their own forms of pasta, from chunky won ton to fine vermicelli. For a dramatic dinner party first course, why not try a delicious clear mushroom soup complete with tiny pasta shapes?

If you make your own pasta dough, the possibilities for making clever soup garnishes are exciting. Stamp out attractive shapes to make clear soups more interesting, or boil, drain, and deep-fry twists, shapes, or noodles to add a crunchy contrast to hearty soups.

Floret Soup

A pretty and delicately flavored soup for a dinner-party menu. Make it in advance and reheat to serve.

SERVES 4–6

2 tbsp butter
2 cloves of garlic, crushed
¾lb tiny broccoli, cauliflower, and romanesco florets
1½ cups dried pastina (any tiny shapes)
5 cups vegetable broth
salt and freshly ground black pepper

1 Melt the butter in a large saucepan, and saute the garlic for about 2 minutes. Add the tiny florets to the garlic and cook for about 5 minutes, stirring occasionally, until tender.

2 Stir the pastina into the floret mixture, cook for 1–2 minutes, then add the vegetable broth. Season with salt and freshly ground black pepper, cover, and bring to the boil.

3 Simmer for about 10 minutes, until the pastina is cooked and the florets have softened. Serve with warm, fresh bread.

Continental Lentil Soup

Canned lentils make this soup even easier to prepare. They are available from most good delicatessens.

SERVES 4–6

¼ cup butter
2 cloves of garlic, crushed
1 cup dried pastina (any tiny shapes)
¼ cup finely chopped, fresh parsley
14oz can brown lentils, drained
6 cups vegetable broth
salt and freshly ground black pepper
freshly grated Parmesan cheese, to serve
  (optional)

1 Melt the butter in a large saucepan and saute the garlic for about 2 minutes, stirring occasionally.

2 Add the pastina and chopped parsley, and stir. Cook for a further 2–3 minutes, then add the lentils and broth, and season with salt and freshly ground black pepper.

3 Bring the soup to the boil, then reduce the heat and simmer for about 15 minutes. Serve with a little freshly grated Parmesan cheese, if you like.

Clear Cep Soup

*This is a formal soup for special occasions. It has a strong mushroom flavor with the
delicate addition of vegetables and pasta to create the contrasting textures.*

SERVES 4

½ cup dried ceps
2½ cups warm water
1 leek
1 carrot
*1 cup conchigliette piccole (tiny pasta
    shells), cooked*
salt and freshly ground black pepper
flat parsley leaves to garnish

1 Place the ceps in the warm water, and leave
to soak for about 30 minutes. Drain the ceps,
reserving the liquid in a saucepan.

2 Slice the ceps, and shred the leek and
carrot. Add the vegetables to the mushroom
stock and cook over medium heat for about 10
minutes, until the vegetables are tender.

3 Add the cooked pasta shells, and season
with salt and freshly ground black pepper.
Cook for a further minute. Serve garnished
with parsley leaves.

Hearty Cream of Mushroom Soup

*Perfect for a cold winter's night or even a filling lunchtime dish. Serve with warm,
crusty garlic bread for a more substantial meal.*

SERVES 4

2 tbsp butter
1 onion, finely chopped
¾lb mushrooms, finely chopped
1tbsp all-purpose flour
2½ cups vegetable broth
1¼ cups milk
salt and freshly ground black pepper
1½ cups cooked tiny pasta shapes
pinch of freshly grated nutmeg

1 Melt the butter in a large saucepan, and
saute the onion for about 3 minutes until
softened. Add the chopped mushrooms, cover,
and cook for a further 5 minutes.

2 Stir in the flour, then gradually add the
broth and milk, stirring well after each
addition. Cover, and cook for 15–20 minutes,
stirring occasionally.

3 Season with salt and freshly ground black
pepper. Stir in the pasta shapes and grated
nutmeg. Cook for a final 2–3 minutes, then
serve.

RIGHT *Clear Cep Soup*

Vegetable and Cilantro Soup

A light, fresh-tasting soup that is ideal either as an appetizer or as a light lunch.

SERVES 4–6

5 cups vegetable broth
2 cups dried pasta (any shape)
dash of olive oil
²⁄₃ cup thinly sliced carrots
1¹⁄₂ cups frozen peas
¹⁄₃ cup chopped cilantro
salt and freshly ground black pepper

1 Bring the vegetable broth to a boil in a large saucepan, and add the pasta with a dash of olive oil. Cook for about 5 minutes, stirring occasionally, then add the sliced carrots.

2 Cook for 5 minutes, then add the peas and cilantro. Season with salt and freshly ground black pepper and simmer gently for about 10 minutes, stirring occasionally, until the pasta and carrots are tender. Serve the soup with finely grated cheese, if you like.

SOUPS

Sprout Soup with Almonds

A warming soup with a subtle flavor, this makes an excellent appetizer for a dinner party. Made up to two days in advance, this soup can be reheated just before serving.

SERVES 4–6

¼ cup butter
1 clove of garlic, crushed
2tsp chopped, fresh rosemary
½lb Brussels sprouts, finely shredded
1½ cups dried ditalini rigati (tiny, short, ridged tubes)
½ cup toasted, flaked almonds
6 cups vegetable broth
salt and freshly ground black pepper
¼ cup light cream
freshly grated Parmesan cheese, to serve

1 Melt the butter in a large saucepan, and saute the garlic and rosemary for about 2 minutes. Add the shredded Brussels sprouts and cook for a further 3–4 minutes, stirring occasionally.

2 Add the ditalini rigati with the flaked almonds. Stir and cook for 1–2 minutes, then stir in the vegetable broth and season with salt and freshly ground black pepper.

3 Cover the soup and simmer for about 10 minutes, stirring occasionally. Stir in the cream, then serve in individual bowls with freshly grated Parmesan cheese.

Red Pepper Soup

This delicious, wholesome, filling soup can be served with your favorite pasta shapes.

SERVES 4

14oz can pimento, drained
2½ cups vegetable broth
salt and freshly ground black pepper
1 tbsp ground coriander
2 cups cooked pasta shapes, such as tortelloni, shells, bows, etc
cilantro, to garnish

1 Place the pimento in a food processor or blender, and puree until smooth. Transfer to a large saucepan and add the vegetable broth, salt and pepper, and ground coriander. Stir and cook over gentle heat for about 10 minutes.

2 Add the cooked pasta shapes and cook for a further 2–3 minutes, until heated through. Serve garnished with cilantro.

Stilton and Broccoli Soup with Tortelloni

A meal in itself, this recipe provides a rich, filling soup, full of flavor.

SERVES 4–6

2 cups fresh tortelloni (choose your favorite filling)
dash of olive oil
¼ cup butter
1 clove of garlic, crushed
1lb broccoli spears, trimmed
5 cups vegetable broth
1 cup crumbled blue cheese
salt and freshly ground black pepper
⅓ cup light cream

1 Bring a large saucepan of water to a boil, and add the tortelloni with a dash of olive oil. Cook for about 5 minutes, stirring occasionally, until tender. Drain and set aside.

2 Melt the butter in a large saucepan, and saute the garlic for about 2 minutes. Add the broccoli spears and continue to cook for about 5 minutes, stirring frequently.

3 Add the vegetable broth to the broccoli mixture, and gradually bring the soup to the boil. Simmer for about 5 minutes, until the broccoli has softened. Puree the soup, in batches if necessary, in a food processor or blender until smooth.

4 Return the soup to the cleaned saucepan, and place over gentle heat. Stir in the crumbled blue cheese, and season with salt and freshly ground black pepper. Cook for about 3 minutes, until the cheese has melted. Stir in the cream and tortelloni. Cook for 2–3 minutes to heat through, then serve immediately.

LEFT *Red Pepper Soup*

Minestrone Soup

There are many different versions of this classic soup; this one is simple, wholesome, and filling. Serve with warm, crusty garlic bread.

SERVES 4–6

1 tbsp extra virgin olive oil
3 cloves of garlic, crushed
1 lb carrots, peeled and finely diced
1 lb zucchini, finely diced
1 cup dried pastina (any tiny pasta shapes)
1/3 cup chopped, fresh parsley
1/4 cup vegetable puree
6 cups good vegetable broth
salt and freshly ground black pepper
freshly grated Parmesan cheese, to serve

1 Heat the olive oil in a large saucepan, and add the garlic. Saute for about 2 minutes, then stir in the diced carrots and zucchini. Cook for about 5 minutes, stirring occasionally.

2 Stir the pastina and chopped parsley into the vegetable mixture, add the vegetable puree and vegetable broth, and season with salt and freshly ground black pepper.

3 Cover and simmer for about 30 minutes, until the vegetables and pasta have softened and the flavors have developed. Serve with freshly grated Parmesan cheese.

Pasta Bean Soup

A nutritious meal in itself — low-fat and full of protein. Serve with warm, crusty garlic bread.

SERVES 4–6

2 tbsp olive oil
3 cloves of garlic, crushed
¼ cup chopped, fresh parsley
1½ cups dried wholewheat gnocchi piccoli (shells)
6 cups vegetable broth
3 tbsp vegetable or tomato paste
14oz can mixed beans, such as borlotti, kidney, cannellini, etc, drained
salt and freshly ground black pepper
freshly grated Parmesan cheese, to serve

1 Heat the olive oil in a large saucepan, and saute the garlic with the chopped parsley for about 2 minutes. Add the gnocchi piccoli and cook for 1–2 minutes, stirring constantly.

2 Pour in the vegetable broth, and add the vegetable or tomato paste. Bring to the boil, reduce the heat, then simmer for about 10 minutes, stirring occasionally, until the pasta is tender.

3 Add the beans, and season with salt and freshly ground black pepper. Continue to cook for a further 5 minutes, then serve with a little freshly grated Parmesan cheese.

CHAPTER THREE

SNACKS AND APPETIZERS

Pasta makes the ideal appetizer as it is so easy to cook in small quantities. It is also great for snacks — quick to prepare, you can have a delicious dish ready in minutes. In this section you will find mushrooms used in cheesy canapés, as a filling for small stuffed pasta rounds, and as the basis for a pasta topping. Or if you prefer tomatoes, how about tomato and mozzarella kebabs, or spicy stuffed tomatoes? Both are delicious and quick to prepare. Other recipes feature peppers, cabbage leaves, zucchini, and green beans in fresh, appetizing combinations.

Pasta-topped Mushrooms

This dish is delicious served cold with a crisp, leafy salad, or warm as an appetizer or an accompaniment. The topping can be made in advance.

SERVES 2–4

½ cup dried small stellette (stars)
dash of olive oil
4 large flat mushrooms
¼ cup butter
1 clove of garlic, crushed
½ yellow pepper, deseeded and finely diced
½ orange pepper, deseeded and finely diced
1 ¼ cups crumbled blue cheese, such as
   Stilton or Danish blue
salt and freshly ground black pepper
2 tbsp chopped, fresh parsley

1 Bring a large saucepan of water to a boil, and add the stellette with a dash of olive oil. Cook for about 7 minutes, stirring occasionally, until tender. Drain and set aside.

2 Cut the stalks out of the mushrooms and discard. Arrange the mushrooms, stalk side up, on a baking sheet and set aside.

3 To make the topping, melt the butter in a frying pan, and saute the garlic for about 2 minutes. Add the diced peppers, and cook for a further 5–7 minutes. Stir in the crumbled blue cheese, and season to taste with salt and freshly ground black pepper. Add the parsley and stellette. Stir well.

4 Top each mushroom with the pasta mixture, then broil for 2–5 minutes, or until the topping is lightly golden and the mushrooms are warmed through.

Deep-fried Mushroom Pasta Pockets

Serve this dish as an appetizer with a small dish of Garlic Mayonnaise (see Tip) for dipping.

SERVES 4–6

½lb fresh lasagna
1 egg, beaten
sunflower oil, for deep-frying

FOR THE FILLING
1 cup cream cheese with herbs and garlic
⅓lb button mushrooms

1 Lay the fresh lasagna out on the work surface, and stamp out rounds using a 3 inch cutter.

2 Place the cream cheese and the mushrooms in a food processor, and blend to form a coarse texture.

3 Spoon some of the mushroom mixture onto one half of each pasta round. Brush a little of the beaten egg around the edges of the rounds, then fold in half to encase the filling, sealing firmly with your fingers. Lay the mushroom pockets out on baking sheets, and chill in the refrigerator for 30 minutes.

4 Heat the oil for deep frying, and fry the mushroom pockets in batches for about 3 minutes, until crisp and golden. Remove from the oil and drain on paper towels. Place on a baking sheet, and keep warm in a low oven until all the batches are cooked. Serve with Garlic Mayonnaise for dipping.

> **GARLIC MAYONNAISE**
> Mix 4 cloves of garlic, crushed, with 1¼ cups mayonnaise. Chill for 30 minutes before serving.

LEFT *Pasta-topped Mushrooms*

Cheesy Mushroom Canapés

These tasty morsels are ideal for entertaining. They can be made in advance, and are delicious served with drinks.

SERVES 8–10

20 dried large lumache rigate or large shells
dash of olive oil
3 tbsp freshly grated Parmesan cheese

FOR THE FILLING
2 tbsp olive oil
1 clove of garlic, chopped
1 small onion, finely chopped
3 tbsp chopped, fresh parsley
1/3lb button mushrooms, very finely chopped
1/2 cup very finely chopped pitted olives
1 cup cream cheese
salt and freshly ground black pepper

1 Bring a large saucepan of water to a boil, and add the pasta with a dash of olive oil. Cook for about 10 minutes, stirring occasionally, until tender. Drain, and rinse under cold running water. Pat dry with paper towels, and set aside.

2 To make the filling, heat the oil in a large frying pan, and saute the garlic and onion for about 3 minutes, until softened. Remove from the heat, and stir in the remaining filling ingredients.

3 Use a teaspoon to stuff each pasta shape with the filling, then arrange them on a baking sheet. Sprinkle with grated Parmesan cheese, and broil for about 5 minutes until golden. Arrange on a serving platter.

Tomato Pasta Timbales

An attractive first course, these timbales are very easy to make and are sure to impress guests. Make them up to one hour in advance and place them in the oven to bake.

SERVES 4

3 cups dried, multi-colored spaghettini
dash of olive oil, plus extra for greasing
4 small tomato slices
2 tbsp tomato pesto
2 eggs, beaten
¼ cup milk
salt and freshly ground black pepper

FOR THE SAUCE
1 cup sieved tomatoes
1 tbsp soy sauce
¼ cup chopped fresh basil
salt and freshly ground black pepper

TO GARNISH
fresh flat parsley sprigs
cherry tomatoes

1 Bring a large saucepan of water to a boil, and add the spaghettini with a dash of olive oil. Cook for about 10 minutes, stirring occasionally, until tender. Drain well.

2 Preheat the oven to 325°F. Grease four 6fl oz individual ovenproof molds with a little olive oil, and place a circle of waxed paper in the bottom of each. Place a slice of tomato in the base of each mold, then carefully pack in the spaghettini, leaving a ¼-inch space at the top.

3 In a small bowl, mix the tomato pesto, eggs, milk, and salt and freshly ground black pepper. Beat well then pour into each spaghettini mold, covering the pasta.

4 Arrange the molds in a roasting pan with enough boiling water to come halfway up the sides. Bake for about 40 minutes, until set and firm to the touch.

5 Meanwhile, to make the sauce, place all the ingredients in a saucepan and heat to simmering point. Simmer for 10 minutes, until thickened slightly.

6 Run a sharp knife around the edges of each timbale, then invert each onto individual plates. Pour a little sauce around each timbale, and garnish.

Tomato Mozzarella Kebabs

*These are excellent for a vegetarian barbecue. Serve the kebabs with plenty of hot,
crusty garlic bread and salad.*

SERVES 4

1 cup dried rotelle (pinwheels)
dash of olive oil, plus ¼ cup
2 cloves of garlic, crushed
salt and freshly ground black pepper
8–12 cherry tomatoes
½lb mozzarella cheese, cut into 1in cubes

1 Bring a large saucepan of water to a boil,
and add the rotelle with a dash of olive oil.
Cook for about 10 minutes, stirring
occasionally, until tender. Drain and rinse
under cold running water. Drain again and set
aside.

2 In a small bowl, combine the olive oil,
garlic, and salt and freshly ground black
pepper. Set aside.

3 To make the kebabs, place one rotelle, a
tomato, then a cube of mozzarella cheese onto
kebab skewers until all the ingredients have
been used. Arrange the skewers on a baking
sheet and brush liberally with the garlic olive
oil mixture, turning the kebabs to coat evenly.

4 Broil the kebabs for 5–7 minutes, turning
the skewers halfway through cooking, until
browned. Serve immediately.

TIP
If using wooden skewers, soak them in
water for at least one hour before
threading on the kebab ingredients. This
will help prevent them from burning
during broiling.

Spaghetti with Cidered Eggs and Gruyère

Break the spaghetti up slightly before cooking it rather than leaving it in long pieces.

SERVES 4

3 tbsp butter
6 shallots or 1 mild white salad onion,
  chopped
1 bay leaf
⅓ cup all-purpose flour
2 cups milk
1¼ cups cider
salt and freshly ground black pepper
1½ cups grated Gruyère cheese
6 eggs, hard-boiled and chopped

1 Melt the butter in a saucepan. Add the
shallots or mild onion and bay leaf. Cook,
stirring, for 10 minutes, then stir in the flour,
and cook for a further 2 minutes.

2 Gradually stir in the milk, and bring to a
boil, stirring all the time. The sauce will be
very thick, but it must thicken before the cider
is added to prevent curdling. Gradually stir in
the cider, and add salt and pepper to taste.
Add the Gruyère, and continue stirring over a
low heat until it has melted.

3 Remove the pan from the heat, stir in the
eggs and spaghetti, and serve at once.

RIGHT *Tomato Mozzarella Kebabs*

Provençal Green Beans with Pasta

Piping hot green beans with freshly grated Parmesan cheese.

SERVES 4–6

2 tbsp olive oil
3 cloves of garlic, crushed
1 onion, chopped
3 tbsp chopped, fresh thyme
1lb green beans
14oz can chopped tomatoes
3 tbsp tomato paste
2 cups vegetable broth
½ cup red wine
salt and freshly ground black pepper
1lb dried pasta (any shapes)
2 tbsp butter
freshly grated Parmesan cheese

1 Heat the oil in a large frying pan, and saute the garlic and onion for about 3 minutes, until softened. Add the thyme, beans, tomatoes, tomato paste, vegetable broth, and wine, season with salt and freshly ground black pepper, and stir well to combine. Cover and cook gently for 25–30 minutes, until the beans are tender. Remove the lid and cook for a further 5–8 minutes, stirring occasionally, until the sauce has thickened slightly.

2 Meanwhile, bring a large saucepan of water to a boil, and add the pasta with a dash of olive oil. Cook for about 10 minutes, stirring occasionally, until tender. Drain and return to the saucepan. Toss in butter and freshly ground black pepper.

3 Serve the beans with the hot, buttered pasta and freshly grated Parmesan cheese.

Stuffed Pasta Shells

These are great as an appetizer or served as a canapé with drinks at a party. They can be made in advance and served cold, or reheated in the oven to serve warm.

SERVES 4–6

12 dried conchiglie rigate (large shells)
dash of olive oil

FOR THE FILLING
1 cup brown lentils, washed
2 cloves of garlic, crushed
14oz can chopped tomatoes
1 tbsp tomato paste
3 tbsp chopped, fresh basil
¼ cup red wine
salt and freshly ground black pepper

FOR THE TOPPING
½ cup fine dried breadcrumbs
⅓ cup finely grated, fresh Parmesan cheese
3 tbsp chopped, fresh parsley

1 Bring a large saucepan of water to a boil, and add the conchiglie rigate with a dash of olive oil. Cook for about 10 minutes, stirring occasionally, until tender. Drain, and rinse under cold running water. Drain again, and lay out on paper towels.

2 To make the filling, bring a large saucepan of water to the boil and add the lentils. Simmer for about 30 minutes, until tender. Drain, and rinse under boiling water.

3 Place the garlic, chopped tomatoes, tomato paste, fresh basil, wine, and salt and freshly ground black pepper in a large frying pan. Bring to boiling point, then reduce the heat and simmer for 2–3 minutes. Add the lentils, stir, and cook for about 10 minutes, until the moisture has evaporated and the mixture has thickened.

4 Use a teaspoon to stuff the pasta shells with the filling mixture, and arrange them on a baking sheet. Combine the topping ingredients in a small bowl, and sprinkle over the stuffed shells. Broil for about 5 minutes, until golden.

Gnocchetti Sardi with Broccoli and Tomatoes

Cook the broccoli as briefly as possible to retain the color and crisp texture.

Serves 4

4 cups dried gnocchetti sardi (small
    dumpling shapes)
dash of olive oil
1/3 cup unsalted butter
3/4lb small broccoli florets
1 clove of garlic, chopped
2 tsp chopped, fresh rosemary
2 tsp chopped, fresh oregano
salt and freshly ground black pepper
7oz can chopped tomatoes
1 tbsp tomato paste
fresh herbs, to garnish

1 Bring a large saucepan of water to a boil, and add the gnocchetti sardi with a dash of olive oil. Cook for about 6 minutes, stirring occasionally, until tender. Drain and return to the saucepan, covered, to keep warm.

2 Meanwhile, melt the butter in a large frying pan. Add the broccoli, garlic, rosemary, and oregano, and season with salt and freshly ground black pepper. Cover and cook gently for about 5 minutes, until tender.

3 Add the chopped tomatoes and tomato paste, and stir. Add the gnocchetti sardi, mix together lightly, then serve immediately, garnished with fresh herbs.

Sweet and Sour Peppers

This excellent appetizer or main course can be served either warm or cold.

Serves 4–6

4 cups dried farfalle (bows)
dash of olive oil, plus 1/4 cup
2 onions, sliced
2 cloves of garlic, crushed
1 1/2lb black peppers, deseeded and cut into
    chunks
1 red pepper, deseeded and cut into strips
2 tbsp brown sugar
1/4 cup raisins
juice of 2 lemons
1/2 cup vegetable broth
salt and freshly ground black pepper
chopped, fresh parsley, to garnish

1 Bring a large saucepan of water to a boil, and add the farfalle with a dash of olive oil. Cook for about 10 minutes, stirring occasionally, until tender. Drain and set aside.

2 Heat the remaining olive oil in a large frying pan, and add the onion and garlic. Saute for about 3 minutes, until the onion has softened.

3 Add the black and red peppers. Stir, cover, and cook over gentle heat for about 10 minutes, stirring occasionally, until the peppers have softened.

4 Stir in the remaining ingredients and simmer, uncovered, for about 5 minutes, stirring occasionally, until the sauce has reduced slightly.

5 Add the cooked farfalle, and stir well to combine. Serve sprinkled with chopped, fresh parsley.

Right *Gnocchetti Sardi with Broccoli and Tomatoes*

Wilted Greens with Fusilli

This quick-to-prepare, nutritious dish is perfect for a light lunch when entertaining friends.

SERVES 4–6

4 cups dried fusilli (small twists)
dash of olive oil
3 tbsp sesame oil
3 cloves of garlic, crushed
¼lb carrots, peeled and cut into ribbons
1 cup shredded young cabbage
5–6 tbsp dark soy sauce
2 tbsp toasted sesame seeds

1 Bring a large saucepan of water to a boil, and add the fusilli with a dash of olive oil. Cook for about 10 minutes, stirring occasionally, until the pasta is tender. Drain thoroughly, and set aside.

2 Heat the sesame oil in a wok or large frying pan, and add the garlic. Stir-fry for 30 seconds, then add the carrot ribbons. Continue to cook for 3–4 minutes, then add the shredded cabbage. Cook for 2–3 minutes, stirring continuously.

3 Stir in the soy sauce, sesame seeds, and the fusilli. Cook for a further 2 minutes, and serve immediately.

TIP

To cut the carrots into wafer-thin ribbons, peel away the outside skin using a vegetable peeler, then continue peeling the carrot.

Pasta-stuffed Cabbage Leaves

This dish can be made the day before serving and kept in the refrigerator. Allow an extra 15–20 minutes to reheat in the oven before serving.

SERVES 4

1 cup dried gnocchetti sardi (dumpling shapes) and/or pastina (any tiny shapes)
dash of olive oil
8 large savoy cabbage leaves, stalks removed

FOR THE FILLING
2 tbsp olive oil
2 cloves of garlic, crushed
2 carrots, peeled and grated
2 zucchini, grated
4 tomatoes, skinned, deseeded, and chopped
1/2 cup chopped walnuts
salt and freshly ground black pepper

FOR THE SAUCE
14oz can chopped tomatoes
1/4 cup red wine
1/2 cup vegetable broth
1 tbsp dried oregano
1 onion, very finely chopped
salt and freshly ground black pepper

1 Bring a large saucepan of water to a boil, and add the pasta with a dash of olive oil. Cook for about 10 minutes, stirring occasionally, until tender. Drain and set aside.

2 Blanch the cabbage leaves in boiling water, then quickly immerse in cold water and drain. Pat dry with paper towels, and set aside.

3 To make the filling, heat the olive oil in a large frying pan and saute the garlic for about 1 minute. Add the grated carrots and zucchini, and cook for a further 3–4 minutes, stirring occasionally, until tender.

4 Add the chopped tomatoes, walnuts, and pasta. Season with salt and freshly ground black pepper. Cook for about 5 minutes, stirring occasionally, then set aside to cool.

5 To make the sauce, place all the ingredients in a saucepan and bring to simmering point. Cook for 20–30 minutes, stirring occasionally, until reduced and thickened. Allow to cool slightly, then transfer to a food processor or blender and puree until smooth. Set aside. Preheat the oven to 400°F.

6 To assemble the stuffed cabbage leaves, lay the blanched leaves out on the work surface, curling upward, and divide the mixture between the leaves, placing it in the center of each. Fold the edges of each leaf over to completely encase the filling, securing with a cocktail stick.

7 Arrange the stuffed leaves in a shallow ovenproof dish, and pour the sauce around the edges. Cover with foil and bake for about 20 minutes, until heated through. Serve immediately, with any extra sauce served separately.

Stuffed Zucchini

A delicious combination of tender zucchini and cilantro mixed with a soy sauce. You can make the filling and the sauce a day in advance. Reheat the sauce while the zucchini are baking.

SERVES 4–6

1 cup broken dried vermicelli (very thin spaghetti)
dash of olive oil
4 medium-sized zucchini
finely chopped walnuts, to garnish

FOR THE FILLING
½ cup soy sauce
1 clove of garlic, crushed
1 cup finely chopped mushrooms
3 tbsp chopped cilantro
¼ cup finely chopped walnuts

FOR THE SAUCE
¼ cup olive oil
2 cloves of garlic, crushed
¼ cup chopped cilantro
salt and freshly ground black pepper
3 tbsp vegetable broth

1 Bring a large saucepan of water to a boil, and add the vermicelli with a dash of olive oil. Cook for about 5 minutes, stirring occasionally, until tender. Drain and set aside.

2 Cut a thin slice lengthwise along the top of each zucchini, and chop this piece finely. Using a teaspoon, scoop out the flesh from the middle of the zucchini and chop roughly. Arrange the hollowed zucchini in a shallow, ovenproof dish and set aside. Preheat the oven to 400°F.

3 To make the filling, place the soy sauce and the garlic in a large frying pan and heat gently. Cook for about 1 minute, then stir in the mushrooms. Cook for about 5 minutes, stirring occasionally, then add the cilantro. Cook for a further 2–3 minutes, then stir in the chopped walnuts and season to taste with salt and freshly ground black pepper. Simmer for 1–2 minutes, then stir in the cooked vermicelli.

4 Remove from the heat and, using a teaspoon, stuff the zucchini with the filling, placing any extra around the zucchini in the dish. Cover the dish with foil and bake for 25–30 minutes, until the zucchini are tender.

5 Meanwhile, to make the sauce, place all the ingredients in a food processor or blender and puree until smooth. Transfer to a small saucepan, and heat gently until warm. Remove the stuffed zucchini from the oven and serve with the cilantro sauce, garnished with finely chopped walnuts.

Sauteed Flageolet Beans with Fusilli

A garlicky dish, made with fresh tarragon to enhance the delicate flavors. Serve as a main course or as an accompaniment.

SERVES 2–4

3 cups dried fusilli (short twists)
dash of olive oil, plus ¼ cup
3 cloves of garlic, crushed
1 large onion, sliced
2 tbsp chopped, fresh tarragon
14oz can flageolet beans, drained
salt and freshly ground black pepper

1 Bring a large saucepan of water to a boil, and add the fusilli with a dash of olive oil. Cook for about 10 minutes, stirring occasionally, until tender. Drain and set aside.

2 Heat the olive oil in a large frying pan and saute the garlic and onion for about 5 minutes, until the onion has browned slightly.

3 Add the tarragon and beans, and season with salt and freshly ground black pepper. Cook for 2–3 minutes, then stir in the fusilli. Cook for 3–5 minutes, to heat through. Serve with a crisp green salad.

Cauliflower and Stilton Terrine

Stilton cheese imparts a rich, creamy taste to this dish.

SERVES 6

1lb cauliflower
¾ cup crumbled blue Stilton cheese
2 cups fresh white bread crumbs
8 green onions, finely chopped
1 tbsp chopped sage
½ cup sour cream
¼ cup dry sherry
2 eggs
salt and freshly ground black pepper
freshly grated nutmeg
butter for greasing
½ quantity spinach-flavored Pasta Dough (page 17) or fresh lasagna verdi
Tomato Sauce (page 19), to serve

1 Cook the cauliflower in boiling water for 5 minutes, then drain well before chopping the florets. Mix the cauliflower, Stilton, breadcrumbs, green onions, sage, sour cream, sherry, and eggs. Add seasoning and nutmeg.

2 Preheat the oven to 350°F. Butter a 2lb loaf pan. Cut the fresh pasta into wide strips which are long enough to line the pan widthwise and overhang the sides. Cook the pasta for 3 minutes, drain, rinse in cold water, then lay out to dry on paper towels.

3 Line the pan completely with bands of pasta, overlapping them neatly, so that some pasta hangs over the rim of the pan. Spread a layer of cauliflower mixture in the base of the pan, then cover with a layer of pasta, cutting it to fit neatly and overlapping pieces as necessary. Continue layering until the pan is full, ending with cauliflower mixture.

4 Fold the ends of the pasta over. Add a final layer of pasta to cover the top of the terrine neatly. Generously butter a piece of waxed paper and lay it on top of the pasta. Cover with foil, sealing it well around the edges of the pan. Stand the pan in a roasting pan and carefully add boiling water to come halfway up the loaf pan. Bake for 1½ hours, until the mixture is firm to the touch and cooked through. Stand for 5 minutes after cooking.

5 Slide a spatula between the pasta and the pan, then invert the terrine onto a flat platter. Use a serrated knife to cut the terrine into thick slices and serve with tomato sauce.

LEFT *Sauteed Flageolet Beans with Fusilli*

CHAPTER FOUR

MOLDS AND BAKES

This chapter points out the versatility of pasta, particularly when the dough is home-made and ready to roll to any shape or size required.

The majority of these recipes are excellent for preparing ahead, so glance through the pages if you are looking for an idea next time you are cooking for friends. Although cooked pasta does not freeze well as a separate ingredient, prepared layered dishes with sauce are terrific freezer candidates. If you are planning on freezing any of the dishes, remember that the freezer life of the finished dish is only as long as the shortest recommended time for the ingredients included in it.

Nutty Mushroom Bake

*Most types of pasta work well for the topping of this dish; try spaghetti or tagliatelle
instead of pennoni.*

SERVES 4

2 cups dried pennoni (quills)
dash of olive oil, plus 2 tbsp
2 tbsp butter
1 onion, chopped
1 clove of garlic, crushed
2 tsp dried oregano
²/₃lb mushrooms, sliced
14oz can chopped tomatoes
2 tbsp tomato paste
¹/₂ cup sliced pimento-stuffed green olives
³/₄ cup roasted cashew nuts
salt and freshly ground black pepper
1 cup grated, mature Cheddar cheese

1 Bring a large saucepan of water to a boil, and add the pennoni with a dash of olive oil. Cook for about 10 minutes, stirring occasionally, until tender. Drain, return to the saucepan, and stir in the butter until melted. Set aside, covered.

2 Preheat the oven to 400°F. Heat the remaining oil in a large frying pan and saute the onion, garlic, and oregano for 3 minutes, or until the onion has softened.

3 Add the sliced mushrooms, and cook for a further 5 minutes, stirring occasionally. Stir in the chopped tomatoes and the tomato paste. Cover, and cook for about 10 minutes, stirring occasionally.

4 Add the sliced olives and the cashews, and season with salt and freshly ground black pepper. Continue to cook for a final 2–3 minutes, then transfer the mixture to a shallow, ovenproof dish. Spoon the buttered pasta on top, and sprinkle with the cheese. Bake for 20 minutes, or until crisp and golden.

Braised Red Cabbage and Pasta Bake

This hearty supper dish for the family is delicious teamed with mashed potatoes.

SERVES 4

2½ cups dried ziti (short macaroni)
dash of olive oil
¼ cup butter
1 onion, chopped
2 cloves of garlic, crushed
1 tbsp chopped, fresh thyme
1lb red cabbage, chopped
½ cup golden raisins
½ cup roasted pine nuts
salt and freshly ground black pepper
1½ cups grated mature Cheddar cheese

1 Bring a large saucepan of water to a boil, and add the ziti with a dash of olive oil. Cook for about 10 minutes, stirring occasionally, until tender. Drain and set aside. Preheat the oven to 400°F.

2 Melt the butter in a large frying pan, and saute the onion, garlic, and thyme for about 3 minutes, until softened. Add the chopped red cabbage, golden raisins, and pine nuts, and season to taste with salt and freshly ground black pepper. Cover and cook for 10 minutes, stirring occasionally, until the cabbage has softened.

3 Stir in the ziti, then transfer the mixture to a shallow, ovenproof dish. Top with the grated Cheddar cheese and bake for about 20 minutes, until golden. Serve immediately.

Cheesy Cauliflower Crumble

Serve with lightly cooked French beans and mashed potatoes for a really satisfying meal.

SERVES 4

1 cup dried pastina (any tiny shapes)
dash of olive oil
2lb cauliflower florets, trimmed
¼ cup butter
salt and freshly ground black pepper

FOR THE TOPPING
¾ cup rolled oats
¾ cup ground filberts
¾ cup ground almonds
1 small onion, very finely chopped
1 clove of garlic, crushed
1 tsp dried thyme
salt and freshly ground black pepper
¼ cup butter
½ cup grated mature Cheddar cheese

1 Bring a large saucepan of water to a boil, and add the pastina with a dash of olive oil. Cook for about 8 minutes, stirring occasionally, until tender. Drain, and rinse under cold running water. Drain again.

2 Place the cauliflower florets in a large saucepan of boiling water and cook for 10–15 minutes, until tender. Drain, reserving the cooking water, and return to the saucepan. Place about a third of the cauliflower and ¼ cup butter in a food processor or blender with enough of the reserved cooking water to make a smooth puree.

3 Stir the cauliflower puree into the remaining florets, and season with salt and pepper. Transfer the cauliflower mixture to a shallow, ovenproof dish and set aside. Preheat the oven to 350°F.

4 To make the topping, place the pastina in a mixing bowl with the rolled oats, ground nuts, onion, garlic, and dried thyme. Season with salt and freshly ground black pepper and rub in ¼ cup butter until the mixture resembles coarse breadcrumbs.

5 Sprinkle the topping over the cauliflower mixture, then scatter the grated cheese on top. Bake for about 35 minutes, until crisp and golden.

Fusilli with Roasted Peppers

To prevent the pasta from sticking together, wash off the starchy cooking liquid by rinsing the pasta under boiling water from the kettle. Continue as directed in the recipe.

SERVES 4–6

1lb dried long fusilli
dash of olive oil
2 yellow peppers, deseeded and cut into chunks
3 cloves of garlic, crushed
¼ cup olive oil
1 cup grated Cheddar cheese
⅔ cup freshly grated Parmesan cheese
chopped, fresh parsley, to garnish

1 Bring a large saucepan of water to a boil, and add the fusilli with a dash of olive oil. Cook for about 10 minutes, stirring occasionally, until tender. Drain, return to the saucepan, and set aside.

2 Arrange the chunks of pepper on a baking sheet and broil for about 5 minutes, or until slightly charred. Preheat the oven to 400°F.

3 Mix the peppers into the pasta with the remaining ingredients, and toss together to combine. Transfer to an ovenproof dish and bake for about 15 minutes, or until heated through and the cheese has melted. Sprinkle with the chopped parsley, and serve.

RIGHT *Fusilli with Roasted Peppers*

Cabbage and Pasta Mold

Serve as an impressive dish for family or friends.

SERVES 4–6

2 cups dried wholewheat macaroni
dash of olive oil, plus extra for greasing
⅓lb small cauliflower florets
1¼ cups Tomato Sauce (page 19)
¼ cup freshly grated Parmesan cheese
½ cup grated, mature Cheddar cheese
2 tbsp chopped, fresh parsley
salt and freshly ground black pepper
5 large green cabbage leaves, stalks removed
fresh herbs, to garnish

1 Bring a large saucepan of water to a boil, and add the macaroni with a dash of olive oil. Cook for about 10 minutes, stirring occasionally, until tender. Drain and set aside.

2 Meanwhile, blanch the cauliflower florets in boiling water, drain, and place in a bowl. Stir in the macaroni, Parmesan and Cheddar cheeses, the Tomato Sauce, and chopped parsley, then season with salt and freshly ground black papper. Allow to cool completely.

3 Preheat the oven to 350°F. Blanch the cabbage leaves in boiling water, then drain and rinse under cold running water immediately. Pat dry with paper towels, then use to line a greased, ovenproof bowl, overlapping the leaves and covering the base. Allow the leaves to hang over the sides of the bowl.

4 Spoon the cool pasta mixture into the prepared bowl, pressing down firmly with the back of the spoon. Fold the overhanging leaves over the top to encase the pasta filling. Cover the top of the bowl with greased foil, and bake in the center of the oven for about 25–30 minutes. Leave to stand for 10 minutes before inverting onto a serving plate. Garnish with fresh herbs, and serve.

Pasta-filled Eggplant

The shells are not eaten, so be sure to scoop out all the soft middle of the eggplants.
A side salad of tomatoes, olives, and croutons on a leafy base is ideal with this dish.

SERVES 4

2 large eggplants (1½lb in weight)
salt and freshly ground black pepper
1 cup soup pasta
¼ cup butter
1 onion, finely chopped
1 cup chopped button mushrooms
½ cup light cream
½ cup grated Parmesan cheese
2 tbsp chopped parsley
2 closed cap mushrooms, sliced, a little
  lemon juice, and a few sprigs of parsley, to
  garnish

1 Cut the eggplant in half, lengthwise, and scoop out the flesh. Reserve the shells, placing them in a gratin dish. Cut the flesh into chunks, and put it into a colander, sprinkling the layers with salt. Set aside over a bowl for 20 minutes, then rinse well, and pat dry. Chop the eggplant flesh finely.

2 Cook the pasta in boiling salted water for about 7 minutes, or according to the instructions on the package until just tender. Melt the butter in a saucepan, and add the onion. Cook, stirring, for 5 minutes. Then add the chopped eggplant and mushrooms, and continue to cook for about 15–20 minutes, or until the vegetables are cooked.

3 Stir in the pasta, cream, Parmesan, and parsley with salt and pepper to taste. Divide this mixture between the eggplant shells, spooning it into them neatly. Broil until they are golden on top.

4 Quickly toss the mushroom slices in lemon juice, top the eggplant with the mushroom slices and sprigs of parsley, and serve at once.

Pinwheel Pasta Bake

A simple, unpretentious dish perfect for a family supper, and makes a good recipe for the freezer. When thawed, reheat, covered, in a medium-hot oven.

SERVES 4–6

1½lb dried rotelle (pinwheels)
dash of olive oil
2 tbsp sunflower oil
1 clove of garlic, crushed
½lb mushrooms, quartered
1 cup chopped zucchini
3 tbsp chopped, fresh parsley
½ cup vegetable broth
1½ cup grated mature Cheddar cheese

1 Bring a large saucepan of water to a boil, and add the rotelle with a dash of olive oil. Cook for about 10 minutes, stirring occasionally, until tender. Drain and set aside.

2 Heat the sunflower oil in a large frying pan, and saute the garlic for 2 minutes. Add the mushrooms and zucchini, and cook, covered, for 5 minutes, or until softened.

3 Stir the chopped parsley and vegetable broth into the mushroom mixture, and continue to cook, covered, for a further 10 minutes. Add the rotelle, and stir in the grated cheese.

4 Preheat the oven to 400°F. Transfer the pasta mixture to a deep casserole dish, and bake for about 20 minutes. Serve with warm, crusty bread.

Tomato Vegetable Crumble

Serve this wholesome main-course dish with lightly cooked French beans tossed in butter and black pepper.

SERVES 4–6

1lb dried macaroni
dash of olive oil, plus 2 tbsp
2 cloves of garlic, crushed
1 onion, chopped
¼ cup chopped, fresh parsley
14oz can chopped tomatoes
½ cup tomato paste
salt and freshly ground black pepper

FOR THE TOPPING
1½ cup rolled oats
¾ cup ground filberts
⅔ cup freshly grated Parmesan cheese
3 tsp dried thyme
⅓ cup butter

1 Bring a large saucepan of water to a boil, and add the macaroni with a dash of olive oil. Cook for about 10 minutes, stirring occasionally, until tender. Drain and set aside.

2 Heat the remaining olive oil in a large frying pan and saute the garlic and onion for about 3 minutes, until softened. Add the parsley, chopped tomatoes, tomato paste, and salt and freshly ground black pepper. Cook for about 5 minutes, then stir in the macaroni. Turn the macaroni mixture into a shallow, ovenproof dish and set aside. Preheat the oven to 350°F.

3 To make the topping, combine all the ingredients in a mixing bowl and rub in the butter until the mixture resembles breadcrumbs. Scatter the topping over the tomato macaroni, and press down gently. Bake for about 30 minutes, until golden and heated through.

LEFT *Pinwheel Pasta Bake*

Bucatini with Tomatoes

*This is a vegetarian version of a simple yet classic Italian dish. Use Parmesan cheese
if Pecorino is not available.*

SERVES 4

4 cups dried bucatini (long tubes)
dash of olive oil
2 cloves of garlic, crushed
1 onion, finely chopped
1lb sieved tomatoes
¼ cup chopped, fresh basil
salt and freshly ground black pepper
butter, for greasing
*⅔ cup freshly grated Pecorino or Parmesan
  cheese*

1 Bring a large saucepan of water to a boil, and add the bucatini with a dash of olive oil. Cook for about 10 minutes, stirring occasionally, until tender. Drain and set aside.

2 Preheat the oven to 400°F. Place the garlic, onion, sieved tomatoes, basil, and salt and freshly ground black pepper in a large frying pan, and heat until simmering. Cook for about 5 minutes, then remove from the heat.

3 Arrange the bucatini in a shallow, buttered, ovenproof dish. Curl it around to fit the dish, adding one or two tubes at a time, until the dish is tightly packed with the pasta.

4 Spoon the tomato mixture over the top, prodding the pasta to ensure the sauce sinks down to the bottom of the dish. Sprinkle with the grated cheese, and bake for 25–30 minutes, until bubbling, crisp, and golden. Cut in wedges, like a cake, to serve.

Spiced Marrow and Pasta Bake

This is also a good recipe for pumpkin.

SERVES 4

2 tbsp butter
1 onion, chopped
1 garlic clove, crushed
1½lb marrow, deseeded, peeled, and cut
    into small cubes
1 tsp mild curry powder
½lb mushrooms, sliced
¼ cup ground almonds
1 tbsp all-purpose flour
2½ cups coconut milk (see Tip)
grated rind of 1 lime
salt and freshly ground black pepper
4 cups pasta spirals, cooked
2½ cups light cream
¼ cup flaked almonds

1 Preheat the oven to 350°F. Melt the butter in a large saucepan. Add the onion and garlic and cook for 5 minutes, then stir in the marrow, curry powder, and mushrooms. Cook for 25–30 minutes, stirring often, until the marrow is tender. Stir in the ground almonds and flour, then pour in the coconut milk, stirring all the time, and bring to simmering point. Remove from the heat and add the lime rind with seasoning to taste.

2 Mix the pasta with the cream and turn half of it into an ovenproof dish or casserole. Spread the pasta out in an even layer, then top with the marrow mixture, then cover with the remaining pasta in an even layer. Sprinkle the almonds over the top and bake for 30 minutes, until lightly browned on top.

TIP

Coconut milk can be made as follows: soak shredded or freshly grated coconut in boiling water, and cover for 30 minutes. Then squeeze out all the liquid by pressing the mixture with a spoon in a strainer. Alternatively, you can buy instant coconut milk powder and dilute it according to the package instructions.

CHAPTER FIVE

CHEESY MAIN DISHES

Add cheese to a pasta dish and you add a whole new dimension to its flavor. With this in mind, here is a collection of recipes that features this incredibly easy-to-use ingredient, whether it be Parmesan, Fontina, Cheddar, or Pecorino cheese. Among the recipes in this section you will find a deliciously creamy mushroom pasta pie; red and yellow peppers filled with a cheesy sauce covered with fresh breadcrumbs baked until crisp and golden; and a cheesy sauce made from Pecorino mixed with cauliflower and broccoli and then added to freshly cooked lasagnette. All equally filling, they are also uncomplicated to make.

Creamy Mushroom Pasta Pie

A dish that is perfect for a romantic dinner for two. It can be made in advance and simply reheated to serve, so you won't be tied to the kitchen.

SERVES 2

1lb puff pastry, thawed if frozen
milk, to glaze

FOR THE FILLING

2 cups dried, wholewheat pasta shells
dash of olive oil
2 tbsp butter
1 clove of garlic, crushed
2 cups sliced button mushrooms
1/2 cup baby corn-on-the-cob, cut into
*   chunks*
1/3 cup all-purpose flour
1/2 cup milk
salt and freshly ground black pepper
1/2 cup grated mature Cheddar cheese
chopped, fresh parsley, to garnish

1 Preheat the oven to 400°F. Roll the pastry out into two rectangular pieces, each measuring 6 x 4 inches. Set one rectangle aside to make the base of the pastry case. Take the other piece and cut out an inner rectangle using a ruler and a sharp knife, leaving a 1in border to make the rim of the pastry case.

2 Reserve the inner rectangle to make the lid and, using a sharp knife, score it to make a pattern. Brush a little milk around the edges of the base of the pastry case, and place the rim in position on top.

3 Place on a baking sheet with the lid alongside, and brush all the surfaces with a little milk to glaze. Bake for about 15–20 minutes, or until well-risen and golden-brown. Remove from the oven, and transfer the pastry case to a wire rack to cool. If the center of the pastry case has risen too high, gently press down to create a hollow space. When cool, place on a serving plate.

4 To make the filling, bring a large saucepan of water to a boil and add the wholewheat pasta shells with a dash of olive oil. Cook for about 10 minutes, stirring occasionally, until tender. Drain well and set aside.

5 Melt the butter in a large saucepan, and saute the garlic, mushrooms, and baby corn-on-the-cob for 5–8 minutes, or until softened. Stir in the flour, and mix to form a paste. Gradually stir in the milk, a little at a time, stirring well after each addition.

6 Bring the sauce slowly to a boil, stirring constantly to prevent lumps from forming. Season with salt and freshly ground black pepper. Stir in the grated cheese and continue to cook for a further 2–3 minutes, until the cheese has melted.

7 Stir the pasta in the sauce, then spoon the sauce into the pastry case. Sprinkle with the chopped, fresh parsley, then place the lid on top and serve.

Fettuccine with Garlicky Creamed Spinach

Serve immediately with plenty of freshly grated Parmesan cheese.

SERVES 4–6

1lb dried fettuccine
dash of olive oil
2 tbsp butter
3 cloves of garlic, crushed
1lb frozen chopped spinach, thawed and
  well drained
1¼ cups light cream
pinch of freshly grated nutmeg
salt and freshly ground black pepper
⅔ cup freshly grated Parmesan cheese, plus
  extra to serve

1 Bring a large saucepan of water to a boil, and add the fettuccine with a dash of olive oil. Cook for about 8 minutes, stirring occasionally, until tender. Drain and set aside, covered, to keep warm.

2 Melt the butter in a large frying pan and saute the garlic for 1–2 minutes, then add the spinach. Cook over medium heat for about 5 minutes, stirring frequently, until the moisture has evaporated.

3 Add the cream and nutmeg, and season with salt and freshly ground black pepper. Toss in the fettuccine and Parmesan cheese, stir, and cook for a final minute. Serve with extra freshly grated Parmesan cheese.

Cheesy Pepper Supper

Based on traditional macaroni and cheese, this colorful supper is a favorite with children.

SERVES 4–6

3 cups dried macaroni
½ red pepper, deseeded and finely diced
½ yellow pepper, deseeded and finely diced
dash of olive oil

FOR THE SAUCE
¼ cup butter
½ cup all-purpose flour
2½ cups milk
2 tsp French mustard
¼ cup grated Cheddar cheese
salt and freshly ground black pepper

FOR THE TOPPING
1 cup fresh breadcrumbs
½ cup grated Cheddar cheese

1 Bring a large saucepan of water to a boil, and add the macaroni with the diced peppers and a dash of olive oil. Cook for about 10 minutes, stirring occasionally, until tender. Drain and transfer to a shallow, ovenproof dish. Set aside. Preheat the oven to 400°F.

2 To make the sauce, melt the butter in a large saucepan, then stir in the flour to make a paste. Gradually stir in the milk, a little at a time, until evenly blended, with no lumps.

3 Gently bring the sauce to a boil, stirring constantly, until thickened. Stir in the mustard and cheese and season with salt and pepper. Continue to cook for a further 1–2 minutes, until the cheese has melted.

4 Pour the cheese sauce over the macaroni and mix it in with a spoon. When the sauce and pasta are evenly combined, sprinkle with the topping ingredients and bake for 25–30 minutes, until crisp and golden.

Lasagnette with Cauliflower and Broccoli

Ask for "mature Pecorino" or "Pecorino Sardo", which are hard cheeses. Alternatively, use Parmesan cheese.

SERVES 6

¾lb dried plain and tomato lasagnette
   (ruffle-edged ribbons)
dash of olive oil, plus 5 tbsp
½lb small cauliflower florets
½lb small broccoli florets
2 cloves of garlic, crushed
1 cup freshly grated Pecorino cheese
pinch of freshly grated nutmeg
2 tbsp chopped, fresh parsley
salt and freshly ground black pepper

1 Bring a large saucepan of water to a boil, and add the lasagnette with a dash of olive oil. Cook for about 10 minutes, stirring occasionally until tender. Drain and set aside, covered.

2 Bring two saucepans of water to a boil, and add the cauliflower to one saucepan and broccoli florets to the other. Cook for about 8–10 minutes, until tender. Drain and set aside.

3 Heat the olive oil in a frying pan, and saute the garlic for about 1 minute. Add the cauliflower, broccoli, lasagnette, about two-thirds of the Pecorino cheese, nutmeg, and parsley, and season with salt and freshly ground black pepper. Mix well, then transfer to a warm serving dish and sprinkle with the remaining Pecorino cheese. Serve immediately.

RIGHT *Lasagnette with Cauliflower and Broccoli*

Farfalle with Fontina

Fontina cheese is available from most good cheese shops and gives this dish a creamy, subtle flavor. Although Emmental cheese is not a perfect substitute, it is more readily available and can be used as a good alternative.

SERVES 4

4 cups dried farfalle (bows)
dash of olive oil
1/3 cup butter
1 onion, finely chopped
3 tbsp chopped, fresh basil
1/2lb mushrooms, sliced
14oz can chopped tomatoes
2 cups coarsely grated Fontina cheese
salt and freshly ground black pepper

1 Bring a large saucepan of water to a boil, and add the farfalle with a dash of olive oil. Cook for about 10 minutes, stirring occasionally, until tender. Drain and set aside, covered, to keep warm.

2 Melt the butter in a large frying pan and saute the onion and basil for about 5 minutes, until the onion is tender, but not browned.

3 Stir the mushrooms into the onion mixture and continue to cook for a further 5–8 minutes, stirring frequently, until the mushrooms begin to brown.

4 Add the chopped tomatoes to the mushroom mixture, and cook for 1–2 minutes. Stir in the cheese, and season to taste with salt and freshly ground black pepper. Cook for a further 3–4 minutes, until the cheese has melted. Serve with the cooked farfalle.

Buckwheat Noodles with Savoy Cabbage

Buckwheat noodles, known as "pizzoccheri," are a speciality of northern Italy, and are available from some Italian delicatessens. Wholewheat or egg tagliatelle make good substitutes.

SERVES 6

3/4lb dried buckwheat noodles
1/2lb savoy cabbage, shredded
1/2lb potatoes, peeled and diced
dash of olive oil
2/3 cup unsalted butter
2 cloves of garlic, chopped
1/4 cup chopped, fresh sage
pinch of freshly grated nutmeg
2 cups diced Fontina cheese
1 1/3 cups freshly grated Parmesan cheese

1 Bring a large saucepan of water to a boil, and add the buckwheat noodles, cabbage, and potato with a dash of olive oil. Cook for 10–15 minutes, stirring occasionally, until tender. Drain and set aside, covered, to keep warm.

2 Meanwhile, melt the butter in a large frying pan, and saute the garlic and sage for about 1 minute. Remove from the heat and set aside.

3 Place a layer of the pasta and vegetables in a warm serving dish, and sprinkle with a little nutmeg, some of the Fontina cheese, and some of the Parmesan cheese.

4 Repeat the layers, then pour the hot garlic butter over the pasta. Mix lightly into the pasta and serve immediately.

CHAPTER SIX

MAIN DISHES

 *The idea behind this chapter is to bring together a range of dishes that are more or less a meal in themselves, with, perhaps, some bread or a salad accompaniment.*

If pasta is added to a liquid already slightly thickened with other ingredients, the cooking time is increased. So, do not be surprised at the length of cooking suggested after the pasta is added to a sauce. Very thick shapes tend to require longer cooking and more water, so thin pasta and small shapes are ideal.

Tagliatelle with Lentil Sauce

Here's a handy recipe you can rustle up in minutes.

SERVES 4

¾lb dried tagliatelle
dash of olive oil
2 tbsp butter

FOR THE SAUCE

2 tbsp olive oil
2 cloves of garlic, crushed
1 large onion, very finely chopped
1 cup red lentils, washed and drained
3 tbsp tomato paste
salt and freshly ground black pepper
2½ cups boiling water
sprigs of fresh rosemary, to garnish
freshly grated Parmesan cheese, to serve

1 Bring a large saucepan of water to a boil, and add the tagliatelle with a dash of olive oil. Cook for about 10 minutes, stirring occasionally, until tender. Drain, and return to the saucepan. Add the butter and stir. Cover and set aside, to keep warm.

2 To make the lentil sauce, heat the olive oil in a large saucepan and saute the garlic and onion for about 5 minutes, stirring occasionally, until softened. Add the lentils, tomato paste, salt and freshly ground black pepper, and stir in the boiling water. Bring to a boil, then simmer for about 20 minutes, stirring occasionally, until the lentils have softened.

3 Reheat the tagliatelle gently for 2–3 minutes, if necessary, then serve with the lentil sauce. Scatter a few sprigs of fresh rosemary over the top, and serve with freshly grated Parmesan cheese.

Tagliatelle with Mushrooms

A quick supper for any occasion. Try using spaghetti or linguini for a change.

SERVES 4

1lb dried tagliatelle
dash of olive oil
2 tbsp butter
1 clove of garlic, crushed
2 tbsp chopped, fresh parsley
2 cups sliced mushrooms
salt and freshly ground black pepper
1¼ cups light cream
freshly grated Parmesan cheese, to serve

1 Bring a large saucepan of water to a boil, and add the tagliatelle with a dash of olive oil. Cook for about 10 minutes, stirring occasionally, until tender. Drain and set aside.

2 Meanwhile, melt the butter in a large frying pan, and saute the garlic and chopped parsley for 2–3 minutes. Add the sliced mushrooms and cook for 5–8 minutes, or until softened and slightly browned.

3 Season the mushroom mixture with salt and freshly ground black pepper, then stir in the cream. Cook the sauce for 1–2 minutes, then stir in the tagliatelle. Continue to cook while stirring to coat the tagliatelle in the sauce. Serve with plenty of freshly grated Parmesan cheese.

RIGHT *Tagliatelle with Lentil Sauce*

Mushroom Stroganoff with Pasta

A rich dinner-party dish that is delicious served with a glass of chilled dry white wine.

SERVES 4—6

¼ cup butter
2 cloves of garlic, crushed
1 onion, sliced into thin wedges
1½lb mixed mushrooms (oyster, maron,
    cup, etc), left whole or cut in half
3 level tbsp all-purpose flour
⅔ cup vegetable broth
3 tbsp dry white wine
salt and freshly ground black pepper
⅓ cup heavy cream
3 tbsp chopped, fresh thyme
2 tbsp paprika
1½lb cooked tagliatelle, tossed in butter,
    to serve

1 Melt the butter in a large saucepan, and saute the garlic and onion for about 7 minutes, until the onion has browned slightly.

2 Add the mushrooms and cook for 2 minutes, then stir in the flour. Cook for 30 seconds, then gradually stir in the vegetable broth, then the wine. Bring the sauce to a boil, and season with salt and freshly ground black pepper. Stir in the cream, fresh thyme, and paprika. Cook for a further 2 minutes, then serve with hot, buttered tagliatelle.

Fusilli with Wild Mushrooms

Wild mushrooms are increasingly available and are the special ingredient in this dish.
Dried ceps can be found in Italian delicatessens; they need to be soaked in water for
30 minutes before using in the recipe.

SERVES 4

4 cups dried long fusilli (twists)
dash of olive oil plus 5 tbsp
1 clove of garlic, crushed
2 tbsp chopped, fresh thyme
2 cups sliced shiitake mushrooms
2 cups fresh oyster mushrooms
¼ cup dried ceps, soaked, drained, and
* sliced*
salt and freshly ground black pepper
freshly grated Parmesan cheese, to serve

1 Bring a large saucepan of water to a boil, and add the fusilli with a dash of olive oil. Cook for about 10 minutes, stirring occasionally, until tender. Drain and set aside, covered.

2 Heat the olive oil in a large frying pan, and add the garlic and fresh thyme. Cook for 1–2 minutes, then stir in all the mushrooms and season to taste with salt and freshly ground black pepper.

3 Fry the mushroom mixture over high heat for 3–4 minutes to brown slightly, then turn the mixture into the saucepan containing the fusilli. Toss together briefly, then serve with a little freshly grated Parmesan cheese.

Spaghettini with Tomato Ragout

This version of ragout is a brilliant standby sauce to use when hunger won't wait for time.

SERVES 4

1lb dried spaghettini
dash of olive oil
freshly grated Parmesan cheese, to serve

FOR THE RAGOUT
2 tbsp butter
1 clove of garlic, crushed
1 large onion, finely chopped
14oz can chopped tomatoes
1¼ cups red wine
¼ cup chopped, fresh basil
salt and freshly ground black pepper

1 Bring a large saucepan of water to a boil, and add the spaghettini with a dash of olive oil. Cook for about 10 minutes, stirring occasionally, until tender. Drain and set aside, covered, to keep warm.

2 To make the ragout, melt the butter in a large frying pan and saute the garlic and onion for about 3 minutes, until softened. Add the remaining ragout ingredients, stir, and simmer for 15 minutes, until slightly thickened. Serve with the spaghettini, sprinkled with freshly grated Parmesan cheese.

Pepper and Pasta Ratatouille

Served with a hot, buttered baked potato, this simple dish is perfectly delicious.

SERVES 4–6

1lb dried wholewheat gnocchi piccoli (small shells)
dash of olive oil, plus 3 tbsp
2 cloves of garlic, crushed
1 onion, chopped
2 green peppers, deseeded and cut into chunks
14oz can chopped tomatoes
3 tbsp tomato paste
½ cup red wine
2 tbsp fresh oregano
salt and freshly ground black pepper
fresh oregano sprigs, to garnish

1 Bring a large saucepan of water to a boil, and add the gnocchi piccoli with a dash of olive oil. Cook for about 10 minutes, stirring occasionally, until tender. Drain and set aside.

2 Heat the remaining olive oil in a large saucepan and saute the garlic and onion for about 3 minutes, until softened. Stir in the pepper chunks. Cover and cook for about 5 minutes, or until the pepper has softened slightly.

3 Stir in the remaining ingredients, except the oregano sprigs, into the pepper mixture and bring to simmering point. Reduce the heat, cover, and cook for about 10 minutes, then stir in the gnocchi piccoli. Cook for a further 5 minutes, stirring occasionally. Serve garnished with fresh oregano sprigs.

RIGHT *Pepper and Pasta Ratatouille*

Pasta al Pomodoro

Any pasta shapes would be suitable for this recipe, so use whatever you have in the cupboard. The sauce is quick and simple, making this dish a perfect supper for unexpected guests.

SERVES 4–6

1lb dried pasta
dash of olive oil
2 tbsp butter
2 cloves of garlic, crushed
1 onion, chopped
1lb sieved tomatoes
salt and freshly ground black pepper
fresh flat parsley sprigs, to garnish
slivers of fresh Parmesan cheese, to serve

1 Bring a saucepan of water to a boil, and add the pasta with a dash of olive oil. Cook for about 10 minutes, stirring occasionally, until tender. Drain and set aside, covered, to keep warm.

2 Melt the butter in a large frying pan, and saute the garlic and onion for about 3 minutes, until softened. Stir in the tomatoes and season with salt and freshly ground black pepper. Simmer the sauce for about 10 minutes then

serve with the pasta, garnished with parsley sprigs and sprinkled with slivers of fresh Parmesan cheese.

TIP
To make slivers of Parmesan cheese, use a vegetable peeler.

= 78 =

Tagliatelle Neapolitan

Yellow tomatoes make this dish look particularly attractive, though red ones taste just as good. If you can't find fresh tagliatelle, use the dried egg version.

SERVES 4

1lb fresh, multi-colored tagliatelle
dash of olive oil, plus 2 tbsp
2 cloves of garlic, crushed
1 onion, chopped
3 tbsp chopped, fresh basil or oregano
1lb yellow and red tomatoes, skinned,
  seeded, and chopped
1 cup sieved tomtoes
salt and freshly ground black pepper
fresh basil, to garnish
freshly grated Parmesan cheese, to serve

1 Bring a large saucepan of water to a boil, and add the tagliatelle with a dash of olive oil. Cook for about 5 minutes, stirring occasionally, until tender. Drain and set aside, covered.

2 Heat the remaining oil in a large frying pan, and saute the garlic, onion, and basil or oregano for about 3 minutes, or until the onion has softened.

3 Add the chopped tomato flesh and sieved tomatoes, and season with salt and freshly ground black pepper. Stir and cook for about 10 minutes, until thickened and bubbling. Serve with the tagliatelle. Garnish with fresh basil and sprinkle with freshly grated Parmesan cheese.

Tri-colored Puree with Pasta

This dinner-party dish can be prepared the day before and kept in the fridge. Reheat the sauces just before serving.

SERVES 4–6

1lb dried spaghetti
dash of olive oil
¼ cup butter
1⅓ cups freshly grated Parmesan cheese
salt and freshly ground black pepper

FOR THE SAUCES

3 red peppers, deseeded and chopped
2 green peppers, deseeded and chopped
1 yellow pepper, deseeded and chopped
4 cups vegetable broth
2 tsp tomato paste
1 tbsp chopped, fresh parsley
½ tsp ground turmeric
salt and freshly ground black pepper

1 Bring a large saucepan of water to a boil, and add the spaghetti with a dash of olive oil. Cook for about 10 minutes, stirring occasionally, until tender. Drain and return to the saucepan. Stir in the butter and Parmesan cheese, and season with salt and freshly ground black pepper. Cover to keep warm, and set aside.

2 To make the sauces, place the red, green, and yellow peppers in a large saucepan and cover with boiling water. Cook for about 10 minutes, then drain.

3 Puree each of the colours separately in a blender or food processor, washing out between colors. Place each color of pepper paste in a mixing bowl, and stir in enough vegetable broth to make the red pepper sauce up to 2½ cups, the green pepper sauce up to 2 cups and the yellow pepper sauce up to 1¼ cups.

4 Stir in the tomato paste into the red pepper sauce, the chopped parsley into the green pepper sauce, and the ground turmeric into the yellow pepper sauce. Season all three sauces with salt and freshly ground black pepper.

5 Transfer the sauces into separate saucepans to reheat, if necessary, then serve with the cheesy spaghetti.

Fusilli with Kidney Beans

The chili flavoring in this dish can be adjusted according to taste.

SERVES 4–6

1lb dried fusilli (short twists)
dash of olive oil
2 x 14oz cans chopped tomatoes
1 onion, sliced
3 tbsp chopped, fresh parsley
pinch of chili powder
salt and freshly ground black pepper
2 tbsp tomato paste
½ cup red wine
14oz can red kidney beans

1 Bring a large saucepan of water to a boil, and add the fusilli with a dash of olive oil. Cook for about 10 minutes, stirring occasionally, until tender. Drain and set aside.

2 Place all the remaining ingredients except the kidney beans in a large frying pan, and bring to boiling point. Reduce the heat and simmer for about 10 minutes, until the liquid has reduced and the onion has softened.

3 Add the fusilli and kidney beans to the tomato mixture. Stir, cover, and cook for about 5 minutes, stirring occasionally. Serve immediately.

RIGHT *Tri-colored Puree with Pasta*

Trenette with Tomato Tarragon Cream

*This rich pasta dish is not for the health conscious! However, it is extremely delicious
with a glass of chilled dry white wine.*

SERVES 4

1lb dried trenette (long, wavy strips)
dash of olive oil, plus 1 tbsp
2 cloves of garlic, crushed
¼ cup chopped, fresh tarragon
8oz cherry tomatoes, halved
1¼ cups light cream
salt and freshly ground black pepper
freshly grated Parmesan cheese, to serve

1 Bring a large saucepan of water to a boil, and add the trenette with a dash of olive oil. Cook for about 10 minutes, stirring occasionally, until tender. Drain, and return to the saucepan. Set aside, covered, to keep warm.

2 Heat the remaining olive oil in a large frying pan and add the garlic, tarragon, and tomatoes. Saute for about 3 minutes, stirring occasionally, then stir in the cream. Season with salt and freshly ground black pepper and cook for 2–3 minutes, until heated through. Stir into the pasta, then serve with freshly grated Parmesan cheese.

Pimento Pasta

A quick recipe to prepare from the cupboard for a last-minute supper surprise.

SERVES 4

¾lb dried spaghettini
dash of olive oil, plus 2 tbsp
2 cloves of garlic, crushed
14oz can red pimento, thinly sliced
salt and freshly ground black pepper
freshly grated Parmesan cheese, to serve
  (optional)

1 Bring a large saucepan of water to a boil, and add the spaghettini with a dash of olive oil. Cook for about 10 minutes, stirring occasionally, until tender. Drain and return to the saucepan. Set aside, covered, to keep warm.

2 Heat the remaining olive oil in a frying pan, and add the garlic and sliced pimento. Stir-fry

for 3–5 minutes, then tip into the warm spaghettini. Stir to combine. Serve with a little freshly grated Parmesan cheese, if desired.

Macaroni Neapolitan

You can make endless variations of this dish by using a different pasta shape each time you prepare it. Serve with a crisp green salad.

SERVES 4

1lb dried macaroni
dash of olive oil, plus ⅓ cup
2 cloves of garlic, crushed
¼ cup chopped, fresh parsley
2 x 1lb cartons sieved tomatoes
1 tbsp tomato paste
salt and freshly ground black pepper
⅓ cup freshly grated Parmesan cheese

1 Bring a large saucepan of water to a boil, and add the macaroni with a dash of olive oil. Cook for about 10 minutes, stirring occasionally, until tender. Drain, and return to the saucepan to keep warm.

2 Preheat the oven to 400°F. Heat the remaining oil in a large frying pan and saute the garlic with the parsley for 2–3 minutes, stirring frequently. Add the tomatoes, tomato paste, and salt and freshly ground black pepper. Cook for about 10 minutes, stirring occasionally.

3 Stir the tomato sauce evenly into the macaroni, then transfer the mixture to an ovenproof dish. Sprinkle the Parmesan cheese over the top, and bake for about 30 minutes.

Italian Spaghettini

Pine nuts give this dish its special taste and texture. Serve it straight from the pan.

SERVES 4

1lb dried, multi-colored spaghettini
dash of olive oil
¼ cup butter
1 clove of garlic, crushed
1 small onion, very finely chopped
¾ cup pine nuts
1 cup sieved tomatoes
salt and freshly ground black pepper
¼ cup chopped, fresh basil
2 tbsp chopped, fresh parsley

1 Bring a large saucepan of water to a boil, and add the dried spaghettini with a dash of olive oil. Cook for about 10 minutes, stirring occasionally, until tender. Drain, and set aside.

2 Melt the butter in a large frying pan and saute the garlic and onion for about 3 minutes, or until the onion has softened. Add the pine nuts and stir-fry until evenly golden.

3 Add the sieved tomatoes, herbs, and salt and freshly ground black pepper, and cook for about 5 minutes, stirring occasionally.

4 Add the spaghettini, and stir well to coat in the tomato sauce. Cook for a further 5 minutes, then serve immediately.

RIGHT Italian Spaghettini

MAIN DISHES

Pepper Pasta Soufflé

*Perfect for an impressive dinnery party. But remember, timing is crucial! Make sure
your guests are seated before removing the soufflé from the oven.*

SERVES 2

¼lb fresh spinach tagliatelle
dash of olive oil, plus 2 tbsp
1 clove of garlic, crushed
½lb mixed colored peppers, deseeded and
   cut into thin strips
2 tbsp chopped, fresh oregano

FOR THE SOUFFLÉ
3 tbsp butter, plus extra for greasing
3 tbsp plain flour
1¾ cups milk
⅓ cup freshly grated Parmesan cheese
4 eggs, separated

1 Bring a large saucepan of water to a boil,
and add the tagliatelle with a dash of olive oil.
Cook for 3–5 minutes, stirring occasionally,
until tender. Drain and roughly chop. Set
aside.

2 Heat the remaining olive oil in a frying pan,
and add the garlic. Cook for 1–2 minutes, then
stir in the pepper strips with the oregano.
Cover and cook over gentle heat for about 10
minutes, stirring occasionally, until the
peppers have softened. Remove from the heat
and set aside. Preheat the oven to 400°F.

3 To make the soufflé, butter two small
soufflé dishes and set aside. Melt the butter in
a saucepan, and stir in the flour to make a
paste. Gradually stir in the milk, then bring the
sauce to the boil, stirring constantly to prevent
lumps, until thickened.

4 Stir in the Parmesan cheese and beat in the
egg yolks, one at a time. Stir in the chopped
tagliatelle until evenly coated.

5 Whisk the egg whites in a clean, dry bowl
until stiff. Fold the egg whites into the
tagliatelle mixture, then divide between the
prepared soufflé dishes. Spoon the pepper
mixture on top of each soufflé, then bake for
20–25 minutes until risen and golden. Serve
immediately.

Bean Curry with Lasagnette

Lasagnette is a longer, thinner version of lasagna. Any form of noodles work well to serve with this recipe.

SERVES 4–6

⅔lb lasagnette (long, thin strips with
    crinkled edges)
dash of olive oil, plus 2 tbsp
2 cloves of garlic, crushed
1 onion, chopped
3–4 tbsp mild curry paste
3 tbsp chopped cilantro
1¼ cups vegetable broth
2 x 14oz cans mixed beans, such as black-
    eyed, flageolet, cannellini, etc., drained
chopped cilantro
lime slices, to garnish

1 Bring a large saucepan of water to a boil, and add the lasagnette with a dash of olive oil. Cook for about 10 minutes, stirring occasionally, until tender. Drain and return to the saucepan. Cover, to keep warm.

2 Heat the remaining olive oil in a large saucepan and saute the garlic and onion for about 5 minutes, stirring occasionally. Stir in the curry paste, and cook for a further 2–3 minutes. Add the chopped cilantro and vegetable broth, and cook for 5 minutes. Stir in the beans, cover, and cook for 10 minutes, stirring occasionally.

3 Serve the curry with the lasagnette, sprinkled with chopped cilantro and garnished with lime slices.

Stuffed Peppers

A refreshing alternative to rice, pasta makes a perfect filling for peppers. Tiny pasta shapes also work well in this dish. Serve with a crisp green salad.

SERVES 4

2¹/₂ cups gnocchetti sardi (small dumpling shapes)
dash of olive oil
4 peppers, for stuffing
flat leaf parsley sprigs, to garnish

FOR THE FILLING
¹/₄ cup butter
6 green onions, finely chopped
2 cloves of garlic, crushed
1 pepper, deseeded and finely diced
salt and freshly ground black pepper
²/₃ cup freshly grated Parmesan cheese

1 Bring a large saucepan of water to a boil, and add the gnocchetti sardi with a dash of olive oil. Cook for about 10 minutes, stirring occasionally, until tender. Drain and set aside.

2 Preheat the oven to 400°F. Lay each pepper on its side and slice off the top, reserving it to make the lid. Scoop out and discard the seeds and pith. Arrange the hollowed-out peppers in a shallow, ovenproof dish, and set aside.

3 To make the filling, melt the butter in a large frying pan and saute the green onions and garlic for about 2 minutes, then add the diced pepper. Season with salt and freshly ground black pepper and cook for about 5 minutes, stirring occasionally.

4 Add the gnocchetti and the Parmesan cheese to the filling mixture, and cook for about 2 minutes to heat through. Using a dessert spoon, stuff each pepper with the pasta filling, scattering any extra around the edges.

5 Place the pepper lids in the dish and bake for about 30 minutes, until the peppers have softened. Just before serving, broil for 2–3 minutes to char the pepper skins, if desired. Serve garnished with parsley sprigs.

Pasta with Green Peppers and Pesto

If linguini is unavailable, spaghettini or tagliatelle will work just as well in this dish.

SERVES 4

1lb fresh linguini (thin, flat strips)
dash of olive oil, plus 2 tbsp
2 cloves of garlic, crushed
½ quantity Pesto Sauce (page 19)
¼ cup vegetable broth
*1 green pepper, deseeded and very thinly
    sliced*
fresh herbs, to garnish

1 Bring a large saucepan of water to a boil, and add the linguini with a dash of olive oil. Cook for about 4 minutes, stirring occasionally, until tender. Drain and return to the saucepan. Stir in a dash more olive oil and set aside, covered, to keep warm.

2 Heat the remaining olive oil in a large frying pan and saute the garlic for 1–2 minutes, then stir in the Pesto Sauce. Add the vegetable broth, stir, and cook for 1 minute, then add the pepper slices.

3 Cook for a further 7–10 minutes, stirring occasionally, until the pepper has softened. Stir the pepper mixture into the linguini and serve, garnished with fresh herbs.

Pasta Paella

Based on the classic recipe, this dish makes a delicious, nutritious alternative, using pasta as the main ingredient. Any pasta shape will do; or use a combination of shapes for extra texture.

SERVES 6–8

1lb dried farfalle (bows)
1 tsp ground turmeric
dash of olive oil, plus 3 tbsp
2 cloves of garlic, crushed
1 Spanish onion
1 red pepper, deseeded and chopped
¼lb baby carrots
¼lb baby corn
¼lb snow peas
¼lb fresh asparagus tips
¾ cup black olives
2 tbsp all-purpose flour

1 Bring a large saucepan of water to a boil, and add the farfalle with the ground turmeric and a dash of olive oil. Cook for about 10 minutes, stirring occasionally, until tender. Drain, reserving the cooking liquid. Set aside.

2 Heat the remaining oil in a large frying pan and saute the garlic and onion for about 3 minutes, until softened. Add the red pepper, carrots, and corn, and stir to combine.

3 Cook for 2–3 minutes, then stir in the snow peas, asparagus tips, black olives, and farfalle. Cook for 2–3 minutes, then sprinkle with the flour and mix it into the vegetable mixture. Cook for 1 minute, then gradually stir in 1½ cups of the reserved pasta cooking liquid. Cook for 2–3 minutes, until the sauce is bubbling and thickened. Serve straight from the pan, or transfer to a warmed serving dish.

Rigatoni with Peppers and Garlic

Raw garlic added at the end gives this dish the true taste of the Mediterranean.

SERVES 4

4 cups dried rigatoni (large tubes)
dash of olive oil, plus ¼ cup
1 large onion, chopped
4 cloves of garlic, finely chopped
2 large red peppers, deseeded and roughly
    chopped
2 large yellow peppers, deseeded and
    roughly chopped
2 tsp chopped, fresh thyme
salt and freshly ground black pepper

1 Bring a large saucepan of water to a boil, and add the rigatoni with a dash of olive oil. Cook for about 10 minutes, stirring occasionally, until tender. Drain and set aside.

2 Heat the remaining oil in a large frying pan. Add the onion, 2 cloves of garlic, peppers, and thyme. Cook over a medium heat for 10–15 minutes, stirring occasionally, until the vegetables are tender and beginning to brown.

3 Add the pasta shapes to the pepper mixture. Stir in the remaining garlic and seasoning. Serve immediately.

Pasta Baskets with Vegetables

The special piece of equipment used in this recipe is known by the French as a nid d'oiseau, *which, loosely translated, means a "bird's nest." It is commonly used to make edible baskets of potato, filo pastry and, in this case, vermicelli.*

SERVES 4

¼lb dried vermicelli
dash of olive oil
vegetable oil, for deep-frying

FOR THE FILLING
2 tbsp sesame oil
2 cloves of garlic, crushed
¼lb baby corn
¼lb snow peas
2 carrots, thinly sliced
3 tbsp soy sauce
1 tbsp toasted sesame seeds

1 Bring a large saucepan of water to a boil, and add the vermicelli with a dash of olive oil. Cook for about 5 minutes, stirring occasionally, until tender. Drain and set aside.

2 Heat the oil for deep frying, and pack the cooked vermicelli into the bird's nest, if using. Otherwise, fry the vermicelli in batches in a frying basket. Cook for 3–5 minutes in hot oil, until the vermicelli is crisp and golden. Remove the basket from the bird's nest, and drain on paper towels. Repeat the process to make three more baskets. Arrange the baskets of loose vermicelli on individual serving plates.

3 To make the filling, heat the sesame oil in a frying pan and saute the garlic for 1–2 minutes. Add the corn, snow peas and carrots, stir, and cook for 3–5 minutes, until tender. Stir in the soya sauce and sprinkle with the sesame seeds. Cook for a further 2 minutes, then spoon into the vermicelli baskets or onto a bed of vermicelli to serve.

RIGHT *Pasta Baskets with Vegetables*

MAIN DISHES

Lentil Pasta Burgers

Served with pitta bread and a little salad, these make a treat for children.

SERVES 2–4

1 cup dried pastina (any tiny shapes)
dash of olive oil
7oz can brown lentils, drained
½ cup dried wholewheat breadcrumbs
⅓ cup finely grated, fresh Parmesan cheese
1 small onion, chopped
1 tbsp chopped, fresh parsley
¼ cup crunchy peanut butter
1 tbsp tomato paste
1 tsp yeast extract
¼ cup hot water
sunflower oil, for shallow frying

1 Bring a large saucepan of water to a boil, and add the pastina with a dash of olive oil. Cook for about 8 minutes, stirring occasionally, until tender. Drain and allow to cool slightly.

2 Combine the pasta in a large mixing bowl with the lentils, breadcrumbs, Parmesan cheese, onion, and parsley.

3 Place the peanut butter, tomato paste and yeast extract in a separate bowl and stir together with the hot water. Add this to the lentil mixture, and mix well.

4 Using damp hands, divide the mixture into four equal portions, and form into burger shapes. Heat the oil for shallow frying, and fry the burgers for about 5 minutes on each side. Serve hot or cold.

TIP

The Lentil Pasta Burgers can also be broiled, if you prefer. Place on a lightly oiled baking sheet, and broil for about 3–5 minutes on each side.

Brassicas with Bavettini

This is a good recipe from the cupboard as any of the brassica family works well here. You could also vary the type of pasta used, according to what you have in your cupboard.

SERVES 4–6

1lb dried bavettini (long flat shapes)
dash of olive oil, plus 3 tbsp
3 cloves of garlic, crushed
1 onion, finely chopped
3 tbsp chopped, fresh rosemary
¾ lb mixed brassicas, such as broccoli, cauliflower, and cabbage, chopped or shredded
salt and freshly ground black pepper
extra olive oil and freshly grated Parmesan cheese, to serve

1 Bring a large saucepan of water to a boil, and add the bavettini with a dash of olive oil. Cook for about 10 minutes, stirring occasionally, until tender. Drain and set aside.

2 Heat the olive oil in a large frying pan and saute the garlic, onion, and rosemary for about 3 minutes, until the onion has softened.

3 Add the chopped or shredded brassicas, and season with salt and freshly ground black pepper. Cook for about 10 minutes, until the vegetables are tender.

4 Toss in the cooked bavettini and cook for about 3 minutes, stirring frequently, until the brassicas have mixed in and the dish is heated through.

5 Serve drizzled with extra olive oil and sprinkled with freshly grated Parmesan.

RIGHT *Lentil Pasta Burgers*

Creamy Leek and Pasta Flan

This dish is delicious both fresh out of the oven or served chilled on a hot summer's day with a crisp green salad.

SERVES 6–8

1½ *cups dried orecchiette (ears)*
dash of olive oil, plus 3 tbsp
a little flour, for dredging
¾lb *puff pastry, thawed if frozen*
2 cloves of garlic, crushed
1lb leeks, washed, trimmed, and cut into
    1in chunks
2 tbsp chopped, fresh thyme
2 eggs, beaten
½ *cup light cream*
salt and freshly ground black pepper
¾ *cup grated Cheddar cheese*

1 Bring a large saucepan of water to a boil, and add the orecchiette with a dash of olive oil. Cook for about 10 minutes, stirring occasionally, until tender. Drain and set aside.

2 Dredge the work surface with a little flour and roll out the pastry. Use to line a greased, 10 inch loose-bottomed, fluted flan ring. Place in the refrigerator to chill for at least 10 minutes.

3 Preheat the oven to 375°F. Heat the remaining olive oil in a large frying pan and saute the garlic, leeks, and thyme for about 5 minutes. Stir in the orecchiette and continue to cook for a further 2–3 minutes.

4 Place the beaten eggs in a small bowl, then whisk in the cream, salt, and black pepper.

5 Transfer the leek and pasta mixture to the pastry case, spreading out evenly. Pour the egg and cream mixture over the top, then sprinkle with cheese. Bake for 30 minutes, until the mixture is firm and the pastry crisp.

Spaghetti with Lentil Balls and Tomato Sauce

This is a great dish for children. Make double the amount of lentil balls and keep them, covered, in the refrigerator for several days for children to snack on. Serve with their favorite pasta for a fast, filling, nutritious dish.

SERVES 4–6

4 cups dried pasta (any shape)
dash of olive oil
sunflower oil, for deep-frying
14oz can chopped tomatoes

FOR THE LENTIL BALLS
½ cup green lentils, washed and drained
¾ cup shelled walnuts or cashew nuts
1 bunch of green onions, chopped
½ cup dried, wholewheat breadcrumbs
1 tbsp curry paste
salt and freshly ground black pepper
2 eggs, beaten

1 Bring a large saucepan of water to a boil, and add the pasta with a dash of olive oil. Cook for about 10 minutes, stirring, occasionally, until tender. Drain and return to the saucepan. Cover to keep warm.

2 To make the Lentil Balls, bring a large saucepan of water to a boil and add the lentils. Simmer for about 25 minutes, stirring occasionally, until softened. Drain well and allow to cool slightly.

3 Place the cooked lentils in a food processor or blender and add the nuts, green onions, breadcrumbs, curry paste, and salt and freshly ground black pepper. Puree until smooth, then gradually beat in the eggs to give a fairly firm mixture. Using slightly damp hands, form tiny balls and set aside on a baking sheet.

4 Heat the oil for deep-frying and cook the balls in batches for about 2 minutes, until crisp and cooked through. Drain on paper towels, then add to the pasta with a can of chopped tomatoes.

5 Place the saucepan over gentle heat to warm through, then serve immediately.

= 97 =

Coconut Vegetables with Pasta

Make this dish a day ahead to allow the flavors to develop.

SERVES 4–6

3 tbsp olive oil
2 cloves of garlic, crushed
1 onion, chopped
2 tsp ground cumin
2 tsp ground coriander
1/2lb creamed coconut, chopped
3 cups boiling water
salt and freshly ground black pepper
1 vegetable broth cube
1 cup diced carrots
1 1/2 cups diced zucchini
5 sticks celery, chopped
1/2 small cauliflower, separated into florets
4oz baby corn
1/3 cup chopped cilantro
3/4lb fresh linguini (thin, flat strips)

1 Heat the olive oil in a large frying pan and saute the garlic, onion, cumin, and coriander for about 3 minutes, stirring occasionally, until the onion has softened.

2 Add the creamed coconut to the boiling water. Stir well and season with salt and freshly ground black pepper. Add the stock cube and stir until dissolved.

3 Add the vegetables and cilantro to the frying pan, and stir well. Cover and simmer for 15–20 minutes, stirring occasionally, until the vegetables are tender. Remove the cover and continue to cook for about 5 minutes, until the sauce has thickened slightly.

4 Meanwhile, bring a large saucepan of water to the boil, and add the linguini with a dash of olive oil. Cook for about 4 minutes, stirring occasionally, until tender. Drain and serve with the vegetables.

Fusilli with Sun-dried Tomatoes

*A dish that is delicious served warm as a main course or cold as a summer salad.
Tomato pesto is widely available.*

SERVES 2–4

1lb dried fusilli (twists)
dash of olive oil, plus extra for drizzling
2 tbsp tomato pesto
6oz jar sun-dried tomatoes, drained and
   chopped
4 tomatoes, sliced into wedges
1/4 cup chopped, fresh basil
salt and freshly ground black pepper

1 Bring a large saucepan of water to a boil, and add the fusilli with a dash of olive oil. Cook for about 10 minutes, stirring occasionally, until tender. Drain and return to the saucepan.

2 Stir in the remaining ingredients, drizzle with olive oil, and serve immediately, or cool and refrigerate to serve chilled, if preferred.

RIGHT *Fusilli with Sun-dried Tomatoes*

CHAPTER SEVEN

STUFFED PASTA

Home-made stuffed pasta really is worth the effort for the quality is evident in the texture of the filling as well as in the flavors. Although it can take a while to get started, once you have a "filling, shaping, and sealing" production line going, and you have the feel for your dough, it is surprising how relaxing stuffing pasta can be . . . rather like eating it, in fact. Before you start to pile up the finished pasta shapes, prepare a large platter or roasting pan for holding them by dusting it with flour. Keep the finished pasta lightly dusted with flour if you have to pile them up, otherwise the shapes will stick together and break. If the dough dries out as you are filling cut pieces, it will be difficult to handle and seal, so keep it loosely covered with plastic wrap. Do not be over-ambitious about the quantity of filling that will fit into small pieces of pasta. Most of the fillings are well seasoned, so a little provides a lot of flavor whereas too much will only split the dough casing during cooking. Brush the dough edges with a little egg but do not make them too wet: this not only makes filling the dough a messy task, but it also causes the two edges to slip apart. Last, remember that the cooking time for stuffed pasta shapes, such as ravioli, depends on the type of filling.

Harvest Moons

These are unusual, filling, and nutritious — good if you like spiced food and ideal for a vegetarian lunch.

SERVES 4

1 tbsp oil
1/2 small onion, chopped
1/2 small carrot, chopped
1 garlic clove, crushed
1 tsp cumin seeds
1 tsp ground coriander
1/2 x 14oz can chick peas, drained
1 tomato, peeled and chopped
2 tsp chopped cilantro
salt and freshly ground black pepper
1/2 quantity turmeric-flavored Pasta Dough
   (page 16)
1 egg, beaten
1/4 cup lightly salted butter
1/2 cucumber, peeled and diced
2 tbsp chopped mint

1 Heat the oil in a small saucepan. Add the onion, carrot, garlic, and cumin seeds. Cook, stirring often, for 10 minutes. Stir in the coriander and cook for 2 minutes, then remove the pan from the heat. Roughly mash the chick peas – they should not be completely smooth. Stir the chick peas into the onion mixture, then add the tomatoes, chopped cilantro and seasoning to taste.

2 Roll out the pasta dough into an 18in square. Use a 2in round cutter to stamp out circles of pasta, dipping the cutter in flour occasionally so that it cuts the dough cleanly. The best way to do this is to stamp all the circles close together in neat lines in the dough, then lift away the unwanted trimmings when the whole sheet is stamped into circles. You should have about 80 circles. Keep the circles which are not actually being used covered with plastic wrap while you fill some of them.

3 Brush a circle of dough with egg, then place some of the chick pea mixture on it. Fold the pasta in half to make a tiny moon-shaped turnover. Pinch the edges of the dough together to seal in the filling. Repeat with the remaining pasta circles. Cook the turnovers in boiling salted water, allowing 3–5 minutes after the water comes back to a boil.

4 While the pasta is cooking, heat the butter. Add the cucumber and mint and set aside over low heat. Turn the cooked pasta into a warmed serving dish and pour the butter and cucumber mixture over. Toss well, then serve at once.

Lentil and Mushroom Cannelloni

The tomato cannelloni is not essential, but adds to the attractive color of the finished dish. Dried cannelloni tubes work just as well.

SERVES 4

¹/₃ quantity Pasta Dough (page 16), with
1 tbsp tomato paste beaten into the eggs
dash of olive oil, plus 3 tbsp
1 cup brown lentils, washed and drained
3 cloves of garlic, crushed
2 tbsp dried thyme
2 x quantity Mushroom Sauce (page 18)
³/₄ cup grated Cheddar cheese
chopped, fresh parsley, to garnish

1 Roll out the Pasta Dough thinly to a 16in square, and cut it into four 4in wide strips. Cut the strips to make 16 squares.

2 Bring a large saucepan of water to a boil, and add the squares of pasta, in batches, with a dash of olive oil. Cook for about 3 minutes, until tender. Drain, and rinse under cold water. Pat dry with paper towels. Set aside.

3 Bring another large saucepan of water to a boil, and add the lentils. Cook for about 30 minutes, stirring occasionally, until tender. Drain and rinse under boiling water. Drain again, and set aside. Preheat the oven to 350°F.

4 Heat the remaining olive oil in a large frying pan, and saute the garlic and thyme for about 2 minutes. Add the lentils, stir, and cook for about 5 minutes. Remove from the heat, and set aside to cool slightly.

5 Place a little of the lentil mixture along one edge of each piece of pasta, and roll up to form a neat tube. Arrange the cannelloni in a shallow, ovenproof dish, seal sides down. Pour the Mushroom Sauce over the cannelloni and sprinkle with grated cheese. Bake for about 40 minutes, until bubbling and golden. Serve garnished with chopped, fresh parsley.

Cannelloni with Greens and Walnuts

Serve with a simple, crisp, fresh salad to complement the rich, cheesy sauce and walnut filling. Fresh spinach is a good alternative for this recipe.

SERVES 4

12 dried cannelloni (tubes)
dash of olive oil
butter, for greasing
½ cup chopped walnuts

FOR THE FILLING
3 tbsp olive oil
1 large onion, chopped
1 clove of garlic, crushed
1lb mustard greens, shredded
7oz can chopped tomatoes
1 tsp dried oregano
3 tbsp chopped, fresh basil
1 cup ricotta cheese
1½ cups fresh, wholewheat breadcrumbs
½ cup walnuts
good pinch of freshly grated nutmeg
salt and freshly ground black pepper

FOR THE CHEESE SAUCE
2 tbsp butter
¼ cup all-purpose flour
1¼ cups milk
½ cup grated Fontina cheese

1 Bring a large saucepan of water to a boil, and add the cannelloni with a dash of olive oil. Cook for about 10 minutes, stirring occasionally, until tender. Drain and rinse under cold running water. Drain again, then pat dry with paper towels and set aside.

2 To make the filling, heat the olive oil in a large frying pan and saute the onion and garlic for 2–3 minutes, until the onion has softened. Add the mustard greens, tomatoes, and oregano. Continue to cook for about 5 minutes, stirring frequently, until the liquid has completely evaporated. Remove from the heat and leave to cool.

3 Place the mustard greens mixture in a food processor or blender, and add the basil, ricotta cheese, breadcrumbs, walnuts, and nutmeg. Puree until smooth, then season with salt and freshly ground black pepper.

4 To make the sauce, melt the butter in a saucepan. Stir in the flour and cook for 1 minute. Gradually stir in the milk, and heat until bubbling and thickened. Stir in the grated Fontina cheese.

5 Preheat the oven to 375°F. Butter the inside of a shallow, ovenproof dish. Using a teaspoon, stuff each cannelloni with the filling, then lay it in the dish.

6 Pour the cheese sauce evenly over the cannelloni. Sprinkle with walnuts and bake for about 30 minutes, until bubbling and golden.

TIP
Sheets of fresh lasagna can be used instead of dried cannelloni. Make up ½ quantity Pasta Dough (page 116), and roll out to ¼in thick. Cut into 4 x 6in rectangles, and spoon some of the filling along the short end of the sheet of pasta. Roll it up into a neat tube, and place in the dish with the sealed end underneath.

Asparagus Roulades

Halve the quantities if you want to serve these as a light first course.

SERVES 4

½ quantity Pasta Dough (page 16)
32 fine asparagus stalks
butter for greasing
½ cup cream cheese
¼ cup freshly grated Parmesan cheese
2 tbsp snipped chives
½ cup fresh breadcrumbs
salt and freshly ground black pepper
1 quantity White Sauce (page 18)

1 Roll out the pasta into a long sheet, slightly larger than 10 x 20in. (If it is more practical, roll out the dough in two batches.) Trim the dough neatly, cut it in half lengthways, then across at 8 equal intervals. This will make 16 rectangles measuring 5 x 2½in. Cook these in boiling salted water for 3 minutes, drain, rinse in cold water, and lay out on double-thick paper towels.

2 Cook the asparagus in boiling salted water for 10–20 minutes, until just tender. Drain and set aside. If you do not have an asparagus pan, use the deepest pan you have and put the asparagus in it so that the tips stand above the rim. Put foil over the top of the pan, crumpling it securely around the rim to seal in the steam.

3 Preheat the oven to 400°F. Butter an ovenproof dish. Mix the cream cheese, half the Parmesan, the chives, and breadcrumbs. Add a little seasoning. Spread or dot a little of the cheese mixture over a piece of pasta, then lay a couple of asparagus stalks on top and roll the pasta over to enclose them. Lay in the dish with the join in the pasta downward. Fill all the pasta in the same way.

4 Pour the White Sauce over the pasta and sprinkle with the remaining Parmesan. Bake for 20–25 minutes, until bubbling hot and lightly browned on top.

Pea-green Ravioli with Cheese Sauce

Fresh mint gives this dish the full flavor it deserves.

SERVES 6

⅔ *quantity Pasta Dough (page 16), omitting the oil and water and adding ⅓ cup spinach liquid instead*
1 *quantity Cheese Sauce (page 18)*

FOR THE FILLING
2 *tbsp olive oil*
1 *onion, very finely chopped*
2 *cups frozen peas*
3 *tbsp chopped, fresh mint*
1 *egg, beaten, for brushing with 2 tsp tomato paste added*
dash of olive oil
fresh mint sprigs, to garnish

1 Keep the fresh Pasta Dough covered with plastic wrap at room temperature and the Cheese Sauce in a saucepan, ready to reheat.

2 To make the ravioli filling, heat the olive oil in a frying pan and saute the onion for about 3 minutes, until softened. Add the frozen peas, cover, and cook for about 7 minutes. Stir in the fresh mint, and remove from the heat. Season with salt and freshly ground black pepper.

3 Allow the filling mixture to cool slightly, then puree in a blender to a slightly coarse texture. Cool completely.

4 To make the ravioli, cut the Pasta Dough in half. Roll out one half to a rectangle slightly larger than 14 x 10in. Trim the edges neatly. Cover with plastic wrap to prevent it drying out. Roll out the other half of the dough to the same measurements, but do not trim the edges. Cover with plastic wrap.

5 Place half teaspoonfuls of the filling mixture in lines, spaced about ¾in apart, all over the trimmed rectangle of Pasta Dough. Brush the beaten egg lightly in lines around the filling mixture, to make the square shapes of the ravioli.

6 Lay the other rectangle of dough on top and, starting at one end, seal in the filling by lightly pressing the dough, pushing out any trapped air, and gently flattening the filling to make little packets. Using a sharp knife or pastry wheel, cut down and across in lines around the filling to make the square ravioli shapes.

7 To cook the ravioli, bring a large saucepan to a boil, and add the ravioli with a dash of olive oil. Cook for about 5 minutes. Drain and set aside, covered, to keep warm.

8 Meanwhile, reheat the Cheese Sauce over gentle heat. Serve with the cooked ravioli and garnish with fresh mint.

TIP

To make ⅓ cup spinach liquid, cook ½lb fresh, chopped spinach leaves, washed and still damp, in a covered saucepan for 5 minutes, stirring frequently. Place the cooked spinach in a sieve, and press out as much green liquid as possible. Add a little extra water to make up the quantity, if necessary.

Mushroom Ravioli

Once you have tasted fresh, home-made ravioli, not only will you never buy it ready-made again, but you will probably want to invest in a ravioli pan, which will make future ravioli-making even easier.

SERVES 6

⅔ quantity Pasta Dough (page 16)
1 quantity Mushroom Sauce (page 18)
1 egg, beaten, for brushing
dash of olive oil
chopped, fresh parsley, to garnish
freshly grated Parmesan cheese, to serve

FOR THE FILLING
2 tbsp olive oil
1 clove of garlic, crushed
3 tbsp chopped, fresh thyme
½lb button mushrooms, finely chopped
2 cups fine, fresh white breadcrumbs
salt and freshly ground black pepper

1 Keep the fresh Pasta Dough covered in plastic wrap at room temperature and the Mushroom Sauce in a saucepan, ready to reheat later.

2 To make the filling, heat the oil in a large frying pan and add the garlic and fresh thyme. Cook for 1–2 minutes, then stir in the mushrooms and fry for 3–5 minutes. Stir in the breadcrumbs, and season to taste with salt and freshly ground black pepper. Remove from the heat and allow to cool completely.

3 To make the ravioli, cut the Pasta Dough in half. Roll out one half to a rectangle slightly larger than 14 x 10 in. Trim the edges of the dough neatly. Cover the rectangle with plastic wrap to prevent it drying out. Roll out the other half of the dough to the same measurements. Do not trim the edges.

4 Place half teaspoonfuls of the filling mixture in lines, spaced about ¾in apart, all over the trimmed rectangle of Pasta Dough. Brush the beaten egg lightly in lines around the filling mixture to make the square shapes for the ravioli.

5 Lay the other rectangle of Pasta Dough on top and, starting at one end, seal in the filling by lightly pressing the dough, pushing out any trapped air and gently flattening the filling, to make little packets. Using a sharp knife or a pastry wheel, cut down and across in lines around the filling to make the square ravioli.

6 To cook the ravioli, bring a large saucepan of water to a boil and add the ravioli with a dash of olive oil. Cook for about 6 minutes, stirring occasionally, until tender. Drain.

7 Meanwhile, reheat the Mushroom Sauce. Serve the Mushroom Ravioli with the Mushroom Sauce, sprinkled with chopped parsley and grated Parmesan cheese.

Three-cheese Cannelloni

Only high-quality Parmesan cheese is suitable for the filling in these cannelloni.

SERVES 4

1/3 quantity Pasta Dough (page 16)
1 cup ricotta cheese
1 cup freshly grated Parmesan cheese
2 cups fresh white breadcrumbs
1 tsp dried oregano
1 bunch watercress, trimmed and chopped
salt and freshly ground black pepper
freshly grated nutmeg
butter for greasing
1 quantity Tomato Sauce (page 19)
1/3lb mozzarella cheese, thinly sliced
handful of basil sprigs

1 Roll out the pasta thinly into a 16in square. Cut it into 4in wide strips, then cut the strips across to make 16 squares. Bring a large pan of salted water to the boil and cook the pieces of pasta, a few at a time if necessary, for 3 minutes. Drain and rinse under cold water, then lay out on double-thick paper towels.

2 Mix the ricotta, Parmesan, breadcrumbs, oregano, and watercress. Add seasoning and a little grated nutmeg to taste, then stir the mixture to make sure all the ingredients are thoroughly combined.

3 Preheat the oven to 400°F. Butter an ovenproof dish. Place some of the cheese mixture on a piece of pasta, then roll it up into a neat tube and place in the dish with the end of the roll underneath. Repeat with the remaining pasta and filling. Ladle the Tomato Sauce over the cannelloni, then top with the mozzarella. Bake for 25–30 minutes, until the cheese has melted and browned. Use scissors to shred the basil leaves and soft stems and sprinkle over the cannelloni. Serve at once.

Cannelloni with Carrot and Zucchini

A fresh, crisp salad is the perfect accompaniment to this dish.

SERVES 4

1/3 quantity Pasta Dough (page 16)
3 tbsp olive oil
1 onion, chopped
1 garlic clove, crushed
1 1/2 cups grated carrots
2/3 cup grated zucchini
1 cup fresh white breadcrumbs
2 tomatoes, peeled and chopped
2 tbsp chopped parsley
1 tsp dried marjoram
salt and freshly ground black pepper
1 quantity Cheese Sauce (page 18)
3 tbsp dry white breadcrumbs

1 Roll out the pasta thinly into a 16in square. Cut it into four 4in wide strips, then cut the strips across four times to make 16 squares. Bring a large pan of salted water to a boil and cook the pieces of pasta, a few at a time if necessary, for 3 minutes. Drain and rinse under cold water, then lay out on double-thick paper towels.

2 Preheat the oven to 350°F. Heat the oil in a large saucepan. Add the onion and garlic and cook for 5 minutes, until the onion is softened but not browned. Stir in the carrots and continue to cook, stirring all the time, for a further 20 minutes, or until the carrots are

tender. Regulate the heat to prevent the carrots from browning. Stir in the zucchini, cook for 2–3 minutes, then remove the pan from the heat. Add the breadcrumbs, tomatoes, parsley, marjoram, and seasoning to taste.

3 Place some of the vegetable mixture on a piece of pasta, then roll it up into a neat tube and place in the dish with the end of the roll underneath. Repeat with the remaining pasta and filling. Pour the cheese sauce over the cannelloni. Sprinkle the breadcrumbs on top and bake for 40 minutes, until golden-brown.

Tomato Tortellini with Tomato Basil Sauce

Although fresh tortellini is increasingly available in supermarkets and delicatessens, nothing tastes quite as good as real home-made pasta. Once the production line is assembled, with the pasta shapes cut out and the filling on standby, the process is simple, efficient, and fun!

SERVES 6–8

⅔ quantity Pasta Dough (page 16) with
  1 tbsp tomato paste beaten into the eggs
1 egg, beaten for brushing
dash of olive oil
chopped, fresh basil, to garnish
freshly grated Parmesan cheese, to serve

FOR THE FILLING
14oz can chopped tomatoes, drained
2 cloves of garlic, crushed
3 cups fresh breadcrumbs
3 tbsp chopped, fresh basil
salt and freshly ground black pepper

FOR THE SAUCE
2 tbsp olive oil
1 clove of garlic, crushed
1 small onion, very finely chopped
14oz can chopped tomatoes
2 tbsp tomato paste
¼ cup chopped, fresh basil
salt and freshly ground black pepper

1 Wrap the Pasta Dough in plastic wrap to prevent it from drying out, and set aside.

2 To make the filling, mix all the ingredients together in a medium-sized bowl and set aside, covered.

3 To make the sauce, heat the olive oil in a large saucepan, and saute the garlic and onion for about 5 minutes, until softened. Add the remaining sauce ingredients and simmer for 10–15 minutes, until bubbling and thickened. Set aside, covered, to keep warm.

4 To make the tortellini, cut the Pasta Dough in half. Keep one portion covered with plastic wrap, and roll out the other portion to a 12in square. Cut the dough into six 2in strips. Now cut the strips into 2in squares, and brush each one with a little beaten egg.

5 Place a little of the tomato filling on each pasta square, then fold the squares over into triangles. Seal the edges, then wrap the long side of the triangle around the tip of your forefinger and pinch the corners together tightly. Continue sealing and shaping the tortellini, then roll out the other half of the pasta dough and repeat the process. Place the filled tortellini on baking sheets lined with waxed paper.

6 To cook the tortellini, bring a large saucepan of water to the boil and add the pasta with a dash of olive oil. Cook for about 5 minutes, stirring occasionally, until tender. Drain and set aside, covered, to keep warm.

7 Reheat the sauce and serve with the tortellini, garnished with chopped, fresh basil and sprinkled with freshly grated Parmesan cheese.

T I P
Do not overfill the tortellini with stuffing or they may split during cooking.

Spinach and Mushroom Lasagna

*Made in advance and put in the oven before the guests arrive, this is the perfect dish
for entertaining. You can relax and enjoy the company while supper sees to itself.*

SERVES 6

butter, for greasing
½lb fresh lasagna noodles
½ quantity Cheese Sauce (page 18)
⅔ cup freshly grated Parmesan cheese

FOR THE FILLING

2 tbsp olive oil
1 clove of garlic, crushed
1 onion, chopped
½lb mushrooms, sliced
*1½lb frozen spinach, thawed and well
  drained*
good pinch of freshly grated nutmeg
2 cups cream cheese
salt and freshly ground black pepper

1 Make the filling first. Heat the olive oil in a large frying pan, and saute the garlic and onion for about 3 minutes. Add the mushrooms and continue to cook for about 5 minutes, stirring occasionally. Add the spinach and nutmeg and cook for about 5 minutes, then stir in the cream cheese and season with salt and freshly ground black pepper. Cook for 3–4 minutes, until the cheese has melted and blended with the spinach mixture. Preheat the oven to 400°F.

2 To assemble the lasagna, butter a lasagna dish and place a layer of lasagna noodles on the bottom. Spoon some of the spinach mixture evenly over it, then add another layer of lasagna. Continue layering the pasta and spinach mixture until both are used up, then pour the Cheese Sauce evenly over the top.

3 Sprinkle the Parmesan cheese over the lasagna and bake for about 40 minutes, until golden and bubbling.

Asparagus Ravioli with Tomato Sauce

A dinner-party dish which can be made in advance — the ravioli can be cooked from frozen. The sauce can be made several hours ahead and reheated before serving.

SERVES 6

²⁄₃ quantity Pasta Dough with 1 tbsp tomato paste beaten into the eggs (page 16–17)
1 quantity Tomato Sauce (page 19)
1 egg, beaten, for brushing
dash of olive oil
chopped, fresh herbs, to garnish

FOR THE FILLING
2 tbsp olive oil
1 clove of garlic, crushed
1 onion, very finely chopped
½lb fresh asparagus, very finely chopped
salt and freshly ground black pepper

1 Keep the fresh Pasta Dough covered with plastic wrap at room temperature, and the Tomato Sauce in a saucepan, ready to reheat before serving.

2 To make the filling, heat the olive oil in a large frying pan and saute the garlic and onion for about 3 minutes, until the onion has softened. Add the chopped, fresh asparagus and season with salt and freshly ground black pepper. Saute the asparagus mixture for about 10 minutes, until softened. Set aside and allow to cool completely.

3 To make the ravioli, cut the Pasta Dough in half. Roll out one half to a rectangle slightly larger than 14 x 10in. Trim the edges of the dough neatly. Cover the rectangle with the plastic wrap to prevent it drying out. Roll out the other half of the dough to the same measurements. Do not trim the edges.

4 Place half teaspoonfuls of the filling mixture in lines, spaced about ¾in apart, all over the trimmed rectangle of Pasta Dough. Lightly brush the beaten egg in lines around the filling mixture, to make the square shapes for the ravioli.

5 Lay the other rectangle of Pasta Dough on top and, starting at one end, seal in the filling by lightly pressing the dough, pushing out any trapped air and gently flattening the filling,

making little packets. Using a sharp knife or pastry wheel, cut down and then across in lines around the filling to make the square ravioli shapes.

6 To cook the ravioli, bring a large saucepan of water to a boil and add the ravioli with a dash of olive oil. Cook for about 6 minutes, stirring occasionally, until tender. Drain and set aside.

7 Meanwhile, reheat the Tomato Sauce. Serve the ravioli with the Tomato Sauce, sprinkled with chopped, fresh herbs.

Lentil and Cilantro Lasagna

You could make up two or three portions and freeze them uncooked. They cook beautifully from frozen at 375°F for 50–60 minutes.

SERVES 1

1/3 cup red lentils, washed and drained
1 onion, roughly chopped
2 cups boiling water
1 tbsp olive oil, plus extra for greasing
1 clove of garlic, crushed
3 tbsp chopped cilantro
1 cup sliced mushrooms
2 tsp soy sauce
1 tbsp tomato paste
salt and freshly ground black pepper
1 sheet fresh lasagna (approx 8 x 4in), cut in half
1/2 quantity Cheese Sauce (page 18)
1/4 cup grated, Cheddar cheese

1 Place the lentils and chopped onion in a large saucepan, and add the boiling water. Bring to the boil, then simmer for about 15 minutes. Drain and set aside. Preheat the oven to 400°F.

2 Heat the olive oil in a large frying pan and saute the garlic and cilantro for about 1 minute, then add the sliced mushrooms. Cook for about 4 minutes, then add the soy sauce and tomato paste, and season with salt and freshly ground black pepper. Add the cooked lentil mixture, stir, and cook gently for about 5 minutes.

3 To assemble the lasagna, oil a shallow ovenproof dish and place one sheet of the lasagna on the bottom. Cover with half the lentil mixture, then add the other sheet of lasagna. Spoon the remaining lentil mixture over the top, spread out evenly, then pour the Cheese Sauce over the top. Sprinkle with grated cheese, then bake for about 20 minutes.

TIP

This is a perfect opportunity to use up any leftover home-made pasta from another recipe – it is not worth making up a fresh batch for this dish since it uses such a small amount.

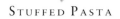

Mushroom Cannelloni

Cannelloni is a time-consuming dish to prepare, but it is always worth the effort.

SERVES 4

8 dried cannelloni tubes
dash of olive oil
butter, for greasing
1 quantity Mushroom Sauce (page 18)

FOR THE FILLING
2 tbsp olive oil
1 clove of garlic, crushed
1 onion, finely chopped
3 tsp chopped, fresh thyme
½lb button mushrooms, finely chopped
1 cup fine, fresh breadcrumbs
salt and freshly ground black pepper

1 Bring a large saucepan of water to a boil, and add the cannelloni with a dash of olive oil. Cook for about 10 minutes, stirring occasionally, until tender. Drain and rinse under cold running water. Pat dry with paper towels and set aside.

2 To make the filling, heat the oil in a large frying pan and saute the garlic, onion, and thyme for about 3 minutes, or until the onion has softened.

3 Add the chopped mushrooms to the onion mixture and continue to cook for about 10 minutes, stirring frequently. Add the breadcrumbs and season with salt and freshly ground black pepper. Stir well.

4 Preheat the oven to 400°F. Butter the inside of an ovenproof casserole dish. Using a teaspoon, stuff each cannelloni with the filling, then lay it in the dish.

5 Pour the Mushroom Sauce evenly over the cannelloni, then bake for about 30 minutes, until heated through and golden on top.

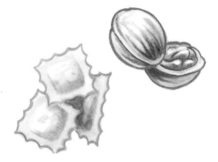

Walnut Cheese Ravioli

The combination of walnut and cheese makes a delicious filling.

SERVES 6

2 tbsp olive oil
1 small onion, finely chopped
1 garlic clove, crushed
1 cup finely chopped walnuts
½ cup ricotta cheese
¾ cup Gruyère cheese
2 tbsp freshly grated Parmesan cheese
6 basil sprigs, finely shredded
1 cup fresh, white breadcrumbs
salt and freshly ground black pepper
⅔ quantity Pasta Dough (page 16)
1 egg, beaten
hot melted butter, to serve
pepper, to serve

1 Heat the oil in a small saucepan. Add the onion and garlic and cook for 15 minutes, until the onion is softened but not browned. Remove from the heat, then stir in the walnuts, ricotta, Gruyère, Parmesan cheese, basil, and breadcrumbs. Add seasoning to taste and mix the ingredients thoroughly.

2 Make the ravioli as on page 113, making sure the mixture is well sealed in the dough. Cook the ravioli for 5 minutes in water that is just boiling. Drain and serve with butter and pepper.

CHAPTER EIGHT

SALADS

 *The recipes in this chapter should inspire new enthusiasm for pasta salads. Bowlfuls of pasta salad can be delicious if the pasta is perfectly "al dente," the other ingredients are complementary, and the dressing brings the whole dish together. I usually prefer pasta shapes in salads but I have also included a couple of ideas for noodles and spaghetti. Making a salad is a good way of using up any leftover pasta dough: cut out your own shapes using cutters or by cutting strips, then squares or diamond shapes. However, avoid ragged shapes and irregular offcuts which can look unappetizing in a salad. If you do cook too much pasta for a meal, turn the surplus into a salad for a picnic or a light lunch the following day.*

Tortellini, Peppers, and Pine Nut Salad

*Red peppers can be used instead of chili peppers, if you prefer. For best results, allow
the salad to chill for at least an hour before serving.*

SERVES 4–6

⅔lb fresh tortellini
dash of olive oil
1 onion, very finely sliced
1 green pepper, deseeded and very finely
    diced
¾ cup toasted pine nuts
1 red chili pepper, deseeded and sliced
    (optional)
4in piece of cucumber, very thinly sliced
1 orange, peeled and very thinly sliced

FOR THE DRESSING
¼ cup olive oil
2 tbsp soy sauce
2 tbsp vinegar
salt and freshly ground black pepper

1 Bring a large saucepan of water to a boil,
and add the tortellini with a dash of olive oil.
Cook for about 4 minutes, stirring
occasionally, until tender. Drain and rinse
under cold running water. Drain again and set
aside.

2 Place the tortellini in a large mixing bowl
and add the remaining salad ingredients. Toss
together lightly.

3 To make the salad dressing, place the
ingredients in a screw-top jar and shake well
to combine. Pour the dressing over the salad,
toss, and serve.

Pasta and Bean Salad

This healthy, high-fiber salad takes only minutes to prepare. Fresh croutons add a crunchy texture.

SERVES 4

½lb spinach-flavored, fresh pasta shapes
½lb French beans, cut into 2in lengths
15oz can flageolet beans, drained
1 red onion, halved and thinly sliced
2 tbsp tarragon vinegar
1 tsp caster sugar
salt and freshly ground black pepper
1 garlic clove, crushed
⅓ cup olive oil
⅓ cup croutons

1 Cook the pasta in boiling salted water for 3 minutes, then drain well. Place the pasta in a bowl. Blanch the French beans in boiling salted water for 3 minutes, then drain them and add them to the pasta. Stir in the flageolet beans and onion, separating the onion as you add them to the salad.

2 Shake the tarragon vinegar, sugar, seasoning, and garlic in a screw-top jar. When the sugar has dissolved add the oil, put the top on the jar and toss well. Pour this dressing over the salad and toss well. Cover and leave until cold.

3 Just before serving, toss the salad and mix in the croutons. Do not leave the salad to stand after the croutons are added or they will lose their crunch.

Eastern Pasta Salad

*A traditional combination of mint and lemon makes this dish a salad for summer.
Choose your favorite pasta shapes for this recipe, and serve with warm pitta bread to
mop up the delicious dressing.*

SERVES 4–6

4 cups dried pasta
dash of olive oil
14oz can chickpeas, drained
¼ cup chopped, fresh mint
finely grated zest of 1 lemon

FOR THE DRESSING
3 cloves of garlic, crushed
⅓ cup extra virgin olive oil
3 tbsp white wine vinegar
freshly squeezed juice of 1 lemon
salt and freshly ground black pepper

1 Bring a large saucepan of water to a boil, and add the pasta with a dash of olive oil. Cook for about 10 minutes, stirring occasionally, until tender. Drain and rinse under cold running water. Drain again, and place in a large mixing bowl.

2 Add the chickpeas, mint, and lemon zest to the pasta. Place all the dressing ingredients in a screw-top jar, and shake well to mix. Pour the dressing over the chickpea mixture and mix well to combine. Cover and chill for at least 30 minutes. Toss before serving.

Pasta and Baked Pepper Salad

Skinning peppers is a boring task but the transformation in flavor is worth the effort. You can use any color combination of peppers. This is another salad that makes a good first course. Instead of shop-bought pasta shapes, you can use your own small pasta squares (pages 12–13).

SERVES 4

3 cups fresh pasta shapes
2 red peppers
1 green pepper
1 yellow pepper
¼ cup olive oil
2 tbsp chopped parsley
1 tbsp lemon juice
salt and freshly ground black pepper
2 eggs, hard-boiled and chopped

1 Cook the pasta in boiling salted water for 3 minutes, drain well, then transfer it to a shallow serving bowl.

2 Grill the peppers until they are scorched all over. This is fairly time-consuming as you have to stand and turn them to make sure that all the skin is blistered. After the skin has lifted away from the pepper flesh it can be peeled off easily and any remains should be rubbed off under cold running water.

3 Dry the peppers on paper towels, halve them; and cut out all their seeds and core. Slice the peppers across into thin strips and scatter them over the pasta. Mix the olive oil, parsley, and lemon juice with seasoning to taste. Use a spoon to trickle the dressing evenly over the peppers and pasta. Sprinkle the chopped hard-boiled eggs over and serve.

Store-cupboard Salad

Use tiny pasta shapes for this salad and serve with warm, crusty French bread.

SERVES 4–6

1½ cups dried pastina (tiny shapes)
dash of olive oil
14oz can mixed beans, such as kidney,
  cannellini, flageolet, etc, drained
1 red pepper, deseeded and very finely diced
2 tsp dried oregano

FOR THE DRESSING
2 cloves of garlic, crushed
¼ cup extra virgin olive oil
2–3 tbsp balsamic vinegar
1 tsp tomato paste
salt and freshly ground black pepper

1 Bring a large saucepan of water to a boil, and add the pastina with a dash of olive oil. Cook for about 8 minutes, stirring occasionally, until tender. Drain and rinse under cold running water. Drain again, and place in a large mixing bowl.

2 Add the beans, red pepper, and oregano to the pasta. Place all the dressing ingredients in a screw-top jar, and shake well to combine. Pour the dressing over the salad, toss, and chill for at least 30 minutes before serving.

Minty Pepper Salad

Serve this cool, light, and refreshing salad for a summer lunch, or make it for a picnic.

SERVES 4

4 cups dried macaroni
dash of olive oil, plus extra for drizzling
1 yellow pepper, deseeded and cut into ½in
  diamonds
1 green pepper, deseeded and cut into ½in
  diamonds
14oz can artichoke hearts, drained and
  quartered
6in piece of cucumber, sliced
handful of mint leaves
salt and freshly ground black pepper
1⅓ cups freshly grated Parmesan cheese

1 Bring a large saucepan of water to a boil, and add the macaroni with a dash of olive oil. Cook for about 10 minutes, stirring occasionally, until tender. Drain and rinse under cold running water. Drain again, then place in a large mixing bowl.

2 Add the remaining ingredients to the pasta and mix well to combine. Drizzle some olive oil over the salad, then serve.

RIGHT *Minty Pepper Salad*

Tagliarini with Green Beans and Garlic

A delicious summer salad, hot main course, or vegetable accompaniment, this dish is suitable for almost any occasion.

SERVES 4–6

¾lb dried tagliarini (flat spaghetti)
dash of olive oil, plus ¼ cup
¾lb haricot beans, topped and tailed
½lb potato, cut into ½in cubes
3 cloves of garlic, chopped
⅓ cup chopped, fresh sage
salt and freshly ground black pepper
freshly grated Parmesan cheese, to serve

1 Bring a large saucepan of water to a boil, and add the tagliarini with a dash of olive oil. Cook for about 10 minutes, stirring occasionally, until tender. Drain and set aside.

2 Cook the beans and potato cubes in a large saucepan of boiling water for about 10 minutes, until tender. Drain well, and set aside to keep warm.

3 Heat the remaining olive oil in a large frying pan, add the garlic and sage, and season with salt and freshly ground black pepper. Saute for 2–3 minutes, then add the cooked beans and potato. Cook for 1–2 minutes, then add the cooked tagliarini and mix well.

4 Cook for about 5 minutes, stirring occasionally, then transfer to a warmed serving dish. Sprinkle with freshly grated Parmesan cheese and serve.

Verdi Vegetables with Vermicelli

A wonderful summer dish to be eaten warm or cold, with chunks of crusty French bread.

SERVES 4–6

¾lb dried vermicelli (long, thin spaghetti)
dash of olive oil
2 tbsp butter
¾lb snow peas, sliced lengthwise
½lb zucchini, shredded lengthwise
¾ cup sliced pimento-stuffed olives
salt and freshly ground black pepper
2 tbsp chopped, fresh parsley
2 tbsp chopped, fresh mint
squeeze of fresh lime juice

TO GARNISH
fresh herbs
lime slices

1 Bring a large saucepan of water to the boil, and add the vermicelli with a dash of olive oil. Cook for about 5 minutes, stirring occasionally, until tender. Drain and set aside.

2 Melt the butter in a large frying pan. Saute the snow peas and zucchini for 5 minutes.

3 Add the remaining ingredients except the lime juice to the vegetable mixture and cook for a further 5 minutes, stirring occasionally. Mix in the vermicelli and cook for 2–3 minutes, until heated through. Squeeze the fresh lime juice over the mixture and serve, garnished with fresh herbs and lime slices.

Herby Mushroom Pasta Salad

*Any small pasta shapes would be suitable for this dish. It can be served as a filling
main course at lunchtime, or as an accompaniment.*

SERVES 4—8

1lb dried pasta shapes
dash of olive oil
½lb mushrooms, quartered
1 red pepper, deseeded and cut into ½in
   squares
1 yellow pepper, deseeded and cut into ½in
   squares
1 cup pitted black olives
¼ cup chopped, fresh basil
2 tbsp chopped, fresh parsley

FOR THE DRESSING

2 tsp red wine vinegar
1 tsp salt
freshly ground black pepper
¼ cup extra virgin olive oil
1 clove of garlic, crushed
1–2 tsp Dijon mustard

1 Bring a large saucepan of water to a boil,
and add the pasta shapes with a dash of olive
oil. Cook for about 10 minutes, stirring
occasionally, until tender. Drain, and rinse
under cold running water. Drain well again.

2 Place the cooked pasta shapes in a large
salad bowl, and add the remaining salad
ingredients. Mix well to combine.

3 To make the dressing, place all the
ingredients in a screw-top jar and shake well.
Pour the dressing over the salad and toss
together. Refrigerate for 30 minutes.

Tomato and Pasta Salad

Orecchiette are small, ear-shaped pasta. If they are not available, gnocchi pasta shapes (dumplings) will work just as well.

SERVES 6–8

1¼lb fresh orecchiette (ears)
dash of olive oil
1lb red and yellow tomatoes, chopped
6in piece cucumber, chopped
¾ cup chopped feta cheese
⅓ cup chopped cilantro
2 tbsp chopped, fresh basil

FOR THE DRESSING
1 tbsp white wine vinegar
¼ cup olive oil
2 cloves of garlic, crushed
salt and freshly ground black pepper

TO GARNISH
cherry tomatoes
cilantro sprigs

1 Bring a large saucepan of water to a boil, and add the orecchiette with a dash of olive oil. Cook for about 5 minutes, stirring occasionally, until tender. Drain and rinse under cold running water. Drain again, and set aside.

2 Place the orecchiette in a large mixing bowl, and add the remaining salad ingredients. Mix to combine. To make the dressing, place all the ingredients in a screw-top jar and shake well. Pour the dressing over the salad and toss to coat. Serve garnished with cherry tomatoes and cilantro sprigs.

CHAPTER NINE

DESSERTS

Finally, a few thoughts on sweet pasta. Depending on your culinary
traditions, you will find this chapter an unexpected pleasure or simply a
mere sample of the recipes that may be created.

Fruit dumplings, dusted with confectioners' sugar and served with sour cream, are
classic examples of the treats from Eastern Europe where they are eaten as a light meal
in their own right. From Italy come fruit compotes and sauces to serve with pasta.

Then there are contemporary creations, such as flavored doughs.

If you plan to serve a substantial dessert, make the main course a light one — or simply
indulge in a mid-afternoon meal instead of lunch one day and make a selection of
sweet filled pasta!

Spiced Apricot Rounds

Orange juice and honey impart a delicious flavor to these fruit rounds, enhanced with slivered almonds.

SERVES 6

1 cup no-soak dried apricots
1 tsp ground cinnamon
2 tbsp powdered sugar
grated peel and juice of 1 orange
⅔ quantity Pasta Dough (page 16)
1 egg, beaten
⅓ cup clear honey
½ cup flaked almonds, toasted
1 tsp cinnamon or allspice
orange slices, to decorate
whipped cream, to serve

1 Mix the apricots, cinnamon or allspice, powdered sugar, and orange peel. Cut the dough in half and roll out one portion into a 12in square. Use a 2in round fluted cutter or a shaped cutter to stamp out pieces of dough. If you work neatly, you will get 36 shapes.

2 Brush a piece of dough with the beaten egg, place a little of the apricot mixture in the middle, then cover with a second piece of dough. Pinch the edges together firmly to seal in the filling. Continue until all the shapes are used, then repeat with the second portion of dough. Place the finished rounds on a plate lightly dusted with cornstarch and keep them loosely covered while you fill the other shapes.

3 Bring a large saucepan of water to a boil and cook the pasta in batches for 5 minutes each. Drain well. While the pasta is cooking, heat the orange juice and honey. Serve the hot pasta coated with the honey and orange juice and sprinkled with the toasted slivered almonds. Decorating individual plates with slices of orange adds a pretty touch. Serve with whipped cream.

Baked Pasta Pudding

This unsophisticated dessert will probably become a firm favorite with the adults as well as children.

SERVES 4

¼lb dried tagliatelle
dash of sunflower oil
¼ cup butter
2 eggs
½ cup sugar
pinch of ground cinnamon
grated zest of 1 lemon
few drops of vanilla extract
¼ cup seedless raisins
sifted powdered sugar, to decorate

1 Preheat the oven to 375°F. Bring a large saucepan of water to a boil, and add the tagliatelle with a dash of sunflower oil. Cook for about 10 minutes, stirring occasionally, until tender. Drain and rinse under cold running water. Drain again and set aside.

2 Place the butter in a shallow, ovenproof dish and melt in the oven for about 5 minutes. Remove from the oven, and carefully swirl the melted butter around the sides of the dish. Set aside to cool slightly.

3 In a mixing bowl, whisk together the eggs and sugar until thick and frothy. Whisk in the cinnamon, lemon zest, vanilla extract, and reserved melted butter. Stir in the seedless raisins and cooked tagliatelle until evenly coated in the egg mixture.

4 Transfer the pudding mixture to the prepared dish and distribute evenly. Bake for about 35–40 minutes until the mixture has set and is crisp and golden. Allow to cool slightly. Serve warm and decorated with sifted powdered sugar.

Rum and Raisin Shapes

Traditional associations of rum and raisins with Christmas make this an ideal alternative dessert to serve at this time.

SERVES 6

½ cup chopped raisins
3 tbsp finely chopped candied peel
1 cup ground almonds
2 tbsp powdered sugar
½ cup rum
⅔ quantity Pasta Dough (page 16)
1 egg, beaten
¾ cup crab apple jelly
¼ cup unsweetened apple juice
2 tbsp finely chopped candied orange peel, to decorate
Greek-style yogurt or cream, to serve

1 Mix the raisins, candied peel, ground almonds, and powdered sugar. Stir in enough of the rum to bind the ingredients together; the rest of the rum is required for the glaze.

2 Roll out, cut, and fill the pasta as for Spiced Apricot Rounds (page 130). When all the pasta is filled, cook in boiling water for 5 minutes and drain well. To make the glaze, gently heat the crab apple jelly with the apple juice until the jelly melts. Bring to a boil, then remove from the heat and stir in the remaining rum.

3 Serve the pasta coated with the apple glaze. Sprinkle with the chopped candied orange peel and offer Greek-style yogurt or cream with the pasta.

DESSERTS

Winter Fruit Compote with Tiny Pasta Shapes

Try this for breakfast. It needs to be started the day before, and will keep for several days in the refrigerator. Make up your own selection of mixed dried fruit, if you prefer.

SERVES 4–6

¼lb dried apricots
¼lb dried apple rings
¼lb dried pears
¼lb dried figs
2oz dried cherries
4 cloves
2 allspice berries
1 stick of cinnamon
finely grated zest and juice of 1 orange
1¼ cups weak tea
½ cup water
1 tbsp soft brown sugar
½ cup dried pastina (any tiny shapes)

1 Place the dried fruit in a bowl with the spices, orange zest, and juice, tea, and water. Cover, and leave to soak overnight.

2 The next day, spoon the compote into a saucepan, bring to the boil, and simmer for 15 minutes, adding a little more water if necessary. Stir in the brown sugar and pastina, and cook for a further 8–10 minutes, until the pastina is tender. Serve warm or cold.

Chocolate Pasta Torte

A decadently rich dessert to serve on special occasions. Use good-quality plain dessert chocolate – ordinary cooking chocolate just won't taste as good.

SERVES 8

⅓lb dried vermicelli (thin spaghetti)
dash of sunflower oil, plus extra for greasing
2 cups broken plain chocolate
¼ cup water
½ cup unsalted butter
½ cup sugar
finely grated zest of 1 orange
8oz can unsweetened chestnut paste
¼ cup brandy
½ cup ground almonds
½ cup flaked almonds
⅓ cup heavy cream
chocolate leaves, to decorate

1 Bring a large saucepan of water to a boil, and add the vermicelli with a dash of sunflower oil. Cook for about 6 minutes, stirring occasionally, until tender. Drain and rinse under cold running water. Drain again and set aside.

2 Lightly oil 7in round springform or loose-bottomed cake pan and line with waxed paper. Lightly oil the paper.

3 Place the water and ⅔ of the chocolate in a small saucepan, and heat gently until melted. Set aside to cool.

4 Meanwhile, cream together the butter, sugar, and orange zest until light and fluffy, then gradually beat in the chestnut paste.

5 Add the melted chocolate to the brandy and mix well. Stir in the almonds and cooked vermicelli. Turn the mixture into the prepared pan and smooth over the surface. Refrigerate overnight.

6 Put the remaining chocolate and the cream into a small bowl over a saucepan of simmering water and heat gently, stirring occasionally, until melted and smooth. Remove the bowl from the heat.

7 Remove the torte from the pan, and place on a wire cooling rack. Pour the melted chocolate mixture evenly over the cake, using a spatula to coat the sides. Leave to set.

8 Carefully transfer the torte to a serving plate and decorate with chocolate leaves.

TIP

To make chocolate leaves, melt ⅓ cup white or milk chocolate in a small bowl over a saucepan of simmering water. Using a small brush, paint the melted chocolate onto the backs of a selection of small leaves. Arrange on a baking sheet lined with waxed paper, and leave to set for at least 2 hours at room temperature. Carefully peel away the leaves and discard.

Fruit Ravioli with a Red Coulis

Look out for dried mango and pineapple in health food shops and delicatessens.
Alternatively, use a mixture of chopped candied fruits in this recipe.

SERVES 6–8

FOR THE FILLING
½ cup finely chopped no-soak dried apricots
½ cup finely chopped dried mango or
  pineapple
finely grated zest of 1 orange
½ tsp ground cinnamon
2 tbsp amaretto liqueur (optional)
⅔ quantity Pasta Dough (page 16),
  (omitting the salt, using 1 tbsp fresh
  orange juice instead of the water, and
  adding the finely grated zest of 1 orange to
  the eggs)
lightly beaten egg
dash of sunflower oil

FOR THE COULIS
2 cups fresh raspberries
½ cup powdered sugar, sifted

TO DECORATE
finely chopped pistachio nuts
fresh raspberries
mint sprigs

1 First make the filling; mix together the apricots, dried mango or pineapple, orange zest, and cinnamon and set aside. Add the amaretto, if desired.

2 To make the ravioli, cut the Pasta Dough in half, and roll out one half to a 14 x 10in rectangle. Trim the edges of the dough, and cover with plastic wrap to prevent it from drying out.

3 Roll out the other piece of Pasta Dough to the same size. Place half teaspoonfuls of the filling mixture in lines ¾in apart on one piece of dough. Lightly brush beaten egg between the filling mixture, and carefully lay the second piece of dough over the top. Starting at one end, press the dough down around the filling, carefully pushing out any trapped air. Using a sharp knife, pastry wheel, or round cutter, cut in lines between the filling to divide the ravioli into squares.

4 Cook the ravioli in a large saucepan of boiling water with a dash of sunflower oil for about 5 minutes, stirring occasionally, until tender. Drain, and set aside to cool slightly.

5 Meanwhile, make the coulis; place the raspberries and powdered sugar in a food processor or blender and puree until smooth. Sieve to remove the seeds.

6 Serve the ravioli on individual plates with the coulis, and decorate with chopped pistachio nuts, raspberries, and mint sprigs.

Chocolate Pasta with Chocolate Sauce

A chocoholic's dream — it has to be tasted to be believed!

SERVES 6

²/₃ quantity Pasta Dough (page 16),
(omitting the salt and adding cocoa
powder and 1oz sugar to the flour)
dash of sunflower oil

FOR THE SAUCE
6oz bar plain chocolate, broken into pieces
¹/₂ cup milk
2 tbsp corn syrup
2 tbsp butter

TO DECORATE
fresh strawberries
amaretti biscuits

1 Keep the Pasta Dough wrapped in plastic wrap to prevent it drying out, and set aside.

2 To make the sauce, place all the ingredients in a small saucepan and heat gently, stirring, for about 5 minutes, until melted, smooth, and shiny. Cool slightly.

3 Roll out the Pasta Dough thinly on a floured surface, and cut into rounds with a 2in round plain or fluted cutter. Pinch the sides of each dough round together, pleating in the middle to make a bow shape. Set the bows aside on baking sheets lined with waxed paper.

4 To cook the pasta bows, bring a large saucepan of water to the boil, and add the pasta with a dash of sunflower oil. Cook for about 3 minutes, stirring occasionally until tender. Drain, and return to the saucepan.

5 Pour the chocolate sauce over the pasta, and stir gently to coat.

Honey, Orange, and Almond Tagliatelle

*Here's a really quick and easy dessert. Pasta tossed in butter and honey syrup makes
a perfect pasta dish to end a meal.*

SERVES 4–6

*½lb dried egg tagliatelle
dash of sunflower oil
4 oranges
⅓ cup clear honey
2 tbsp granulated brown sugar
1 tbsp lemon juice
3 tbsp butter
¾ cup flaked almonds*

1 Bring a large saucepan of water to a boil, and add the tagliatelle with a dash of sunflower oil. Cook for about 8–10 minutes, stirring occasionally, until tender. Drain and set aside.

2 While the pasta is cooking, peel and slice three of the oranges, and cut the slices in half. Squeeze the juice from the remaining orange into a small saucepan. Add the honey, sugar, and lemon juice. Bring to a boil, stirring to dissolve the sugar, and simmer for 1–2 minutes, until syrupy.

3 Melt the butter in a large frying pan, and fry the flaked almonds until golden. Stir in the tagliatelle and honey syrup, heat through, then quickly stir in the orange slices. Serve immediately.

TIP

Pare strips of zest from the skin of one orange, and cut into thin "julienne" strips for decoration.

Cinnamon Fettuccine with Apple and Cinnamon Sauce

This delightful autumn dessert is delicious served with cream. Ground mixed spice makes a good alternative to cinnamon.

SERVES 6

²⁄₃ *quantity Pasta Dough (page 16),*
 (omitting the salt and adding 2 tsp ground cinnamon to the flour)

FOR THE SAUCE
1lb dessert apples, peeled, cored, and sliced
finely grated zest of 1 lemon
¼ tsp ground cinnamon
3 tbsp water, plus ½ cup
2 tbsp granulated light brown sugar
½ cup golden raisins
1 tbsp butter, plus a little extra
2 tsp cornstarch blended with 2 tsp cold water
flour, to dredge
dash of sunflower oil

1 Keep the Pasta Dough wrapped in plastic wrap to prevent it from drying out, and set aside.

2 To make the sauce, put the apples into a saucepan with the lemon zest, cinnamon, and 3 tbsp water. Cover, and cook gently until the apples have softened. Remove about half of the apple slices from the saucepan, and set aside. Place the remaining apples in a food processor or blender, and puree until smooth.

3 Return the puree to the saucepan and stir in the reserved apples, sugar, golden raisins, 1 tbsp butter, cornstarch mixture, and ½ cup water. Cook for 5 minutes, stirring constantly, until bubbling and thickened. Set aside.

4 To make the fettuccine, roll out the pasta dough very thinly on a floured surface. Lightly dredge with flour, then roll up and use a sharp knife to cut the dough into ¼-inch wide slices. Shake out the noodles as they are cut, and pile them on a floured baking tray.

5 To cook the fettuccine, bring a large saucepan of water to a boil and add the pasta with a dash of sunflower oil. Cook for about 3 minutes, stirring occasionally, until tender.

6 Meanwhile, reheat the sauce. Drain the fettuccine, and toss with a little extra butter. Stir in the sauce, and serve on warmed individual plates.

TIP

For a special occasion, sprinkle each plate of pasta with a little calvados or rum before serving.

Glossary of Italian Pasta

AGNELLOTTI, AGNOLLOTTI OR AGNOLOTTI (1)
Cushions of stuffed pasta, round or semi-circular, attributed to Piedmont region.

AGNOLINI
Small ravioli.

AMORI/AMORINI (2a & b)
Knots. They do not resemble knots, but are hollow spirals that may be ridged.

ANELLINI
Tiny rings, for use in soups.

BAVETTE
Oval spaghetti.

BIGNI
Local name for spaghetti.

BIGOLI
A type of spaghetti.

BUCATINI (3)
Thick, hollow spaghetti.

CAMPANELLE (4)
Bells. Small cones of pasta with frilly edges. Good for trapping sauce.

CANDELE (5)
Meaning candles, the pasta shapes are, in fact, pipes, about ½–¾ inch in diameter.

CANNELLE
Meaning pipes, and including cannellini, cannolicchi, cannelloni, and canneroni.

CANNELLONI
Popular pipe shapes, used for stuffing, coating with sauce, and baking.

CANNERONI (6)
Larger than canneroncini, these are short pasta tubes.

CANNERONCINI (7)
Short lengths (about ½ inch) of narrow pipes.

CAPELLINI (8)
Thin hairs. Very fine spaghetti.

CAPELLINI SPEZZIATI (9)
Short, broken lengths of capellini.

CAPPELLETTI (10)
Little hats. Small circles of pasta indented in the center or with a pinched pleat, forming a hat shape.

CASARECCIA (11)
Slightly twisted lengths of "S"-shaped pasta.

CASONSEI
Stuffed rings of pasta from Bergamo.

CICATELLI DI SAN SEVERO (12)
One of a range of hand-made pasta from the Puglia region. These opaque, white, curled shaves of pasta are made from wheat flour and water, but no egg. They swell significantly on cooking.

CONCHIGLIE (13 & 15)
Shells. They come in many sizes, from conchigliette, for soup, to large conchiglioni, for stuffing.

CONCHIGLIE RIGATE (14)
Large shells with a ridged texture. Ideal for boiling, draining, stuffing, and baking or broiling with a gratina topping.

CORALLINI (16)
Tiny soup pasta that look like little slices of hollow spaghetti.

DITALI (17)
Meaning thimbles, these are short lengths of hollow tube, slightly smaller than the end of your little finger. Good for salads and for a chunkier pasta in soup.

DITALINI (19)
Smaller than ditali both in length and diameter, with proportionally thicker pasta.

FARFALLE (20)
Butterflies. The term "bows" is also sometimes used for the same pasta shape. Made from thin, flat pasta, these shapes tend to cook quickly for their size. Good for adding to layered (moist) dishes in which the pasta is cooked from raw.

FARFALLINI (21)
Wonderful, tiny farfalle, for soups or when small shapes are required. Very decorative.

FETTUCCINE (22a & b)
Flat noodles. This is the alternative Roman name for tagliatelle. Readily available fresh.

FISCHIETTI (18)
Little whistles. Thin macaroni.

FRESINE (23)
Straight noodles, slightly narrower than tagliatelle and in similar lengths to short spaghetti.

FUSILLI (24)
Spirals, which may be long or short depending on the region of origin. Apparently, they were originally made by wrapping spaghetti around knitting needles, which gives some indication of the size and thickness of the pasta.

FUSILLIER COL BUCO (25)
Long, slim spirals (about the same length as short spaghetti).

GNOCCHETTO (29)
More yellow in color than gnocchetti, ridged, and semi-tubular in shape. Look more like an average pasta shape than the more gnocchi-like types of dried pasta.

GNOCCHI (30)
Little dumplings. The dried pastas are shaped to resemble gnocchi which are marked with a fork. There are many types of fresh gnocchi.

GOMITI
Hollow corners of pasta, like elbows, lumache (small), or pipe.

GRAMIGNA
Couch grass. Pasta shaped like grass.

LASAGNETTE (33)
Small lasagna. The same as malfade, this is a type of wide ribbon noodle with frilly edges.

LE EMILIANE
A name for nests of pappardelle.

LINGUINE
Little tongues. Narrow noodles or flat spaghetti, readily available fresh.

LUNETTE
A term used on some brands of semi-circular stuffed pasta.

MACARONI OR MACCHERONI (36)
Hollow tubes of pasta, larger than spaghetti. Originally sold in long lengths, wrapped in blue paper packages, and still available as such from better delis. Quick-cook, short-cut macaroni and elbow macaroni (another term for elbows or slightly longer right angles) are the most popular and readily available types. This was once the generic name for a limited range of early pasta types, especially those used by the British.

MACCHERONCINI
Very small macaroni.

MACCHERONI RIGATI
Ribbed macaroni.

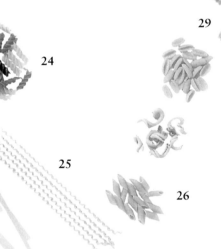

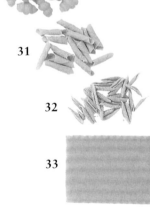

GENOVESINI (26)
Presumably attributed in origin to Genoa, these are short, diagonally cut lengths of fairly thick tube pasta. Rather like short, plump penne.

GLI STROZZAPRETI (27)
The basic shape as casareccia, but the cut lengths are curled around into "C" or "S" shapes.

GNOCCHETTI SARDI (28)
Small versions of gnocchi, they are ridged, opaque, and pale in color.

I GARGANELLI ROMAGNOLI (31)
Squares of pasta rolled diagonally to make slim rolls with pointed ends.

IS MALLOREDDUS LUNGHI (32)
Like small, pale (creamy white), distinctively ridged gnocchetti but tightly curled.

LASAGNA
Wide strips or squares of pasta. Available fresh or dried.

LUMACHE (34a & b)
Snails. Available in different sizes, the large ones are ideal for stuffing. I also found this name attributed to ridged shell shapes – presumably snail shells!

LUMANCHINE (35)
Small snail shapes as above, but not as distinctive in shape. For salads, stuffing vegetables (peppers) or when a reasonably chunky soup is required.

MAFALDE (37)
Wide, flat noodles with fluted or ruffled edges.

MAFALDINE
Flat noodles with fluted or ruffled edges, narrower than mafalde.

MALFATTINI
Finely chopped.

MISTA PASTA (38)
Mixed pasta. Mixed shapes sold together.

MISTO CORTO (39)
Mis-shapen. A mixture of tubes, spaghetti, and broken pieces of similar length.

NIDI (40)
Nests. Small, rounded bundles of tagliatelle or fettuccine, these unravel when cooked. Pasta nests as a base for serving a sauce are created by arranging the cooked pasta in a nest shape on the plate.

OFFELLE
Stuffed pasta of ravioli type from Trieste.

ORECCHIETTE (41)
Little ears. Opaque pasta, paler than usual shapes and slightly thicker than some. With a slightly softer texture when cooked, ideal for rich sauces (vegetable ragouts). Look as though they have been formed as the result of someone pressing their thumb into a piece of pasta.

PAGLIA E FIENO (42a & b)
Straw and hay. Green and white linguine or very narrow flat noodles mixed together. Also available as pink and white, flavored with tomato and plain.

PANSOTTI
Stuffed pasta of Ligurian origins, usually triangular.

PAPPARDELLE (43)
Wide, ribbon egg noodles.

PASTA A RISO (44)
Pasta in the shape of small grains of rice. This cooks quickly and may be used instead of the Greek equivalent, known as orzo or minestra.

PASTINE
Small pasta shapes; soup pasta.

PENNE (45)
Quills. Hollow pasta cut into short lengths, at a slant.

PENNE, MEZZANI (46)
Small penne, slimmer and slightly shorter.

PENNE, MEZZANINE (47)
Yet smaller penne, shorter and slimmer than both the above.

PERCIATELLI
Thick, hollow spaghetti, thicker than bucatini.

PERLINE
Little pearls. Small soup pasta.

QUADRETTI
Small squares of pasta for soup.

RADIATORI (48)
Radiators. Deeply ridged, pale pasta like old-fashioned radiators.

RAVIOLI
Small, stuffed pasta shapes. May be square or round, depending on their region of origin.

RIGATONI (49)
Ridged tubes, like large ridged macaroni. Good for baked dishes.

RUOTI (50)
Wheels. Cartwheel shapes.

SEDANI
Ridged, curved tubes of macaroni type, resembling celery stalks.

SPAGELLINI (51)
Short, thin pieces of spaghetti.

SPAGHETTI (52)
Long, slim, solid pasta. The majority is now shorter than it used to be, but it is still available in long, blue packages.

SPIGANARDA (53)
Similar to pasta a riso, but consists of longer grains.

STELLINE (54)
Tiny stars. Soup pasta.

TAGLIATELLE (55)
Familiar ribbon noodles. *See also* Fettuccine.

TORCHIETTI (56)
Small torches. Slightly swirled lengths of ridged pasta.

TORTELLINI (57a & b)
Stuffed pasta, formed from squares or circles, filled and folded in half, then pinched together into rings.

TORTIGLIONI (58)
Ridged tubes, like rigatoni, but curved, with the ridges forming a slightly spiral on the pasta.

TRENETTE
Finer than linguine or similar to flattened spaghetti.

TUBETTI (59)
Small tubes. Small, short lengths of hollow pasta.

VERMICELLI
Thin worms. The Neapolitan term for spaghetti, which is slightly thicker than the familiar form. However, on an international basis, this is the term ascribed to fine spaghetti.

ZITI (60)
Spinsters or bachelors. Thick macaroni.

ZITONI (61)
Thicker than ziti.

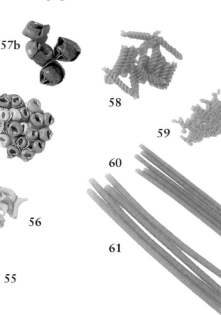

Index

INDEX